RISING TO THE
CHALLENGE

ALSO BY CARLY FIORINA

Tough Choices

CARLY FIORINA

RISING TO THE CHALLENGE

■ ■ ■

My Leadership Journey

SENTINEL

SENTINEL

Published by the Penguin Publishing Group
Penguin Random House LLC
375 Hudson Street
New York, New York 10014

USA | Canada | UK | Ireland | Australia | New Zealand | India | South Africa | China
penguin.com
A Penguin Random House Company

First published by Sentinel, an imprint of Penguin Publishing Group, a division of
Penguin Random House LLC, 2015

ISBN 978-1-59184-803-5

Printed in the United States of America
1   3   5   7   9   10   8   6   4   2

Set in Palatino

Penguin is committed to publishing works of quality and integrity. In that spirit, we are
proud to offer this book to our readers; however, the story, the experiences, and the
words are the author's alone.

To Lori, who is forever in our hearts.
We miss you every day.

Contents

Prologue
1

C H A P T E R 1
The Power of Human Potential
9

C H A P T E R 2
A Soul Intact
25

C H A P T E R 3
Cancer
57

C H A P T E R 4
Annus Horribilis
77

C H A P T E R 5
Meet Me in Mendota
91

CHAPTER 6

A Cautionary Tale

119

CHAPTER 7

What Women Want

135

CHAPTER 8

Unlocking America's Potential

153

Epilogue

183

Acknowledgments

189

Index

191

RISING TO THE CHALLENGE

Prologue

THE TWO POLICE OFFICERS STOOD AWK-
wardly in our living room. They shifted uncom-
fortably, as if worried that the mud on their boots might
soil the light carpet. What was really bothering them,
though, was the news they had to deliver. Frank and I
looked at them and knew they had something terrible to
say. Hope is a curiously strong thing and so we hoped
that what they had to tell us wasn't what we feared.

They asked us to sit down. Frank collapsed in a chair. I
sat on the carpet next to him, my arms wrapped around
his knees. The police officers said our daughter was
dead, three thousand miles away. We hadn't heard from
her in a couple of weeks. Frank had been in touch with

the volunteer paramedics he had worked with in New Jersey, and they asked the police to check on her. She was thirty-four years old. At that moment, we lost both the woman she was and the woman she could have been. All our hope for her and her life died. Frank and I leaned into each other and sobbed, for Lori, for our family, for ourselves. A heart truly can feel as though it is breaking apart into a thousand shattered pieces.

The news wasn't completely unexpected. Lori had been battling addictions for years. She had been in and out of rehab three times. As anyone who has loved someone with an addiction knows, you can force someone into rehab, but you can't make her well. Only the addict can do that. Lori couldn't—or wouldn't—take that first step of admitting she was powerless over her addiction. And ultimately her body just gave out.

I had known her since she was six years old. I fell in love with her and her big sister, Tracy, almost before I fell in love with their father, my husband, Frank. They were little angels, both to be with and to behold. Tracy was a brunette, and looked like her father. Lori had long blond hair and bright, sparkling eyes. We came into each other's lives just when we needed each other the most. Lori was a bouncy, happy, and loving child. I was a manager at AT&T, eager for a family. In Frank and Tracy and Lori, I found my family.

All young people represent potential, but Lori had more than most. She was smart and hardworking. Whatever she did, whether it was tending bar or marketing pharmaceuticals, she was the best. And more important, Lori was a kind, compassionate soul. On Frank's birthday one year, while Lori was in college, he was busy in court giving a deposition until late at night. When he got home after midnight, Lori was waiting for him. She and a girlfriend had decorated the house for his birthday. She had a tremendous amount to give—brains, talent, but most of all, love.

We worried that Lori drank too much in college, but we didn't think she had an addiction. Those were good years—or so they seemed at the time. I had taken Lori around to visit different campuses, and she had settled on Fairleigh Dickinson, near our home in New Jersey. She lived with us while she went to school. She did well academically and thrived socially. After graduation she toyed with the idea of going on to graduate school but got an offer for a job in sales at a pharmaceutical company. It was a good job, but at first she didn't want to take it—she didn't think she would succeed. She ended up being great at it.

What we didn't know until much later was that behind the scenes in those seemingly happy, high-functioning years, Lori began abusing prescription drugs. Not long after graduation she got her own apartment, met a man, and eventually got married. Her marriage would take her to Richmond, Virginia, for a time. There her drug use got worse. Like so many high-achieving young women, Lori also struggled with bulimia for years. Despite her repeated stays in rehab, the combination of bulimia, alcoholism, and drug abuse took its toll. She was divorced and living in New Jersey when she died.

Virtually every minute of every day after those two police officers stood in our living room, Frank and I wondered what signs we had missed, what we could have done differently to help Lori overcome her demons. It is the torture of second-guessing that every parent who has lost a child to addiction goes through. What breaks my heart the most, though, is the look that grew in Lori's eyes as her addictions overcame her. There is an old saying, "The eyes are the windows to the soul." As Lori grew progressively sicker, the potential-filled girl I knew disappeared from behind her eyes. The light, the sparkle she once had, left her. What remained was a dull, flat void. It was the look of hopelessness. And that look is what haunts me most.

Only faith, family, and friends got me through those first terrible days after Lori's death. Without my complete conviction that a loving God had been with Lori, and was with our family as we buried her, I am not sure how I would have coped. Each time, when grief, guilt, and regret threatened to overcome me, I would do as I have always done since my childhood. I whispered the Lord's Prayer in my mind. Now, I added the Twenty-third Psalm to my daily prayers: "The Lord is my shepherd, I shall not want. Yea, though I walk through the valley of the shadow of death, I will fear no evil, for Thou art with me."

Frank seemed destroyed and so I was not surprised when, soon after Lori's funeral, he came to me and told me he had lost his faith. I prayed nightly that he would be given a sign and his faith restored. It was months later, just days before Father's Day 2010, when it happened. He had been in the garage changing the oil in his car. A pile of boxes, which had been stored for years in the corner, caught his eye. For no particular reason he decided to open one of them. Lying on top were four Father's Day cards from Lori. In one of those cards was a long letter she had written to him many years ago, telling him what a fine father he was and how much she loved him. He read "I love you" in her childish handwriting. He approached me with tears and relief in his eyes and those cards in his hand. He knew, once again, that Jesus loved him and that Lori had found peace. But in those days of spiritual isolation, Frank, too, had that flat, hopeless look in his eyes. I've come to know that when people don't have hope (and faith, among other things, gives us hope), the look is always the same.

Later, when I ran for the U.S. Senate in California, I saw this look in the eyes of more people than I should have. I found myself in a town named Mendota, in California's Central Valley, once part of the most productive farmland in the world, now known as the Appalachia of the West. I met three men who used to work the fields in

Mendota. Now they were out of work along with almost 40 percent of their fellow residents. It wasn't just that they had no jobs. As I looked around town I saw the fields of almond trees the men used to tend now had become desiccated wastelands. Trees lay uprooted in dead, shriveled heaps. And flowing through the middle of all this parched destruction was a rushing aqueduct. Men and women in suits, thousands of miles away, had decided that this water couldn't be used to give life to the fields. Men and women in suits had decided these men couldn't work—the farmworkers' potential was less important than Washington's ideological agenda. The men I met in Mendota also had that flat, lifeless look in their eyes. The look of hopelessness. The look of potential unfulfilled.

Whenever someone introduces me at a speech or an event, they read off the lines of my biography and I am always struck by how neat and tidy—even effortless—it sounds. As if life were a series of happy, easy successes. Life isn't that, of course. I know that I am blessed in many ways, but I've had setbacks; I've known tragedy and struggle. Losing Lori is first among them. And her death came less than two weeks after I had completed a grueling treatment for breast cancer. Experiencing the worst pain that a parent can endure tested my faith. It humbled me with the realization that I could not protect her, or save her, or fix her pain and suffering. Lori's death and my battle with cancer taught me that there is so much we cannot control. Yet I came to see lessons and blessings in these passages. I know now that life is not measured in time. Life is measured in love and positive contributions and moments of grace.

Lori's potential was never fulfilled but death is not the only thing that crushes potential. Too many people lose hope for themselves. Too many lack the opportunity to use their God-given gifts. Like Lori, every person has far more potential than they realize. Every person has the capacity to live a life of meaning, dignity, and purpose.

What I also know is that Americans are failing to achieve their potential today. One in six Americans lives in poverty. More Americans are on food stamps than at any time in our history. Record numbers of Americans remain unemployed. Underemployment is a growing problem. Labor force participation rates are at historic lows. Reversing over 200 years of belief in the American Dream, most Americans now believe their children's futures will be diminished.

Some survey this bleak landscape and see the signposts on the road of the inevitable decline of America. Some see a nation of "takers." Many see victims in need of care by benevolent big government.

Me? I think of Lori, and I see an ocean of untapped potential.

CHAPTER 1

The Power of
Human Potential

I T WAS A STRANGER AT A ROTARY CLUB MEET-
ing in the "live free or die" state of New Hampshire
who would almost perfectly distill my thoughts about
America today.

I was about to give a speech to a room full of people of
all political persuasions. As I ate lunch prior to the
speech, a gentleman at my table told me he was a Democrat. "I don't think we're going to agree," he said. I
thought about that for a moment, thanked him for his
candor, and asked him to hear me out. Then I began my
speech. Americans agree on a lot of things, but we seem
to spend all of our political discourse arguing with great

vitriol about our disagreements. "I want to talk to you today about what we all agree on," I said.

It is worthwhile to consider who we are as Americans, I continued. And I told my story—a story only possible in America. When I was a young girl, my mother—who was also my Sunday school teacher one year—gave our class a small plaque. It read: "What you are is God's gift to you. What you make of yourself is your gift to God."

Those words stayed with me. I graduated from college with a degree in medieval history and philosophy. Both my degree and the recession of the time made me unemployable, so I enrolled in law school. My father was thrilled, but I hated it. I quit after a single semester. I needed to earn a living, so I answered the want ads and took the first job I was offered. I went to work full time doing what I had done part time to help put myself through college: typing and answering the phones. I worked as a secretary at a little, nine-person firm in Palo Alto.

"I have traveled all over the world. I have lived in many places in the world," I told that New Hampshire Rotary Club. "And I know that only in America is it possible for a young woman to start out as a secretary and become the CEO of the largest technology company in the world."

America is the greatest nation on earth because that story isn't just my story—it is the story of every dreamer, every striver, every law school dropout and medieval history major who ever realized her potential in America. We are a nation founded on a visionary and, at the time, radical idea. That visionary idea is that every human life has potential, and everyone has the right to fulfill his or her potential. That is what the Founders meant when they wrote "life, liberty and the pursuit of happiness."

Human potential is the one truly limitless resource we have. There are all kinds of reasons why people fail to fulfill their potential. Perhaps they lack opportunity or support. Perhaps they lack tools or training or education. Perhaps they are in desperate and destitute circumstances in which no one will give them the dignity or the respect they deserve. Perhaps in some cases they might lack courage. But everyone has potential. This I know. Our Founders knew it too. They had the radical insight that the right to fulfill your potential—to use your God-given gifts—is a right that comes from God and cannot be taken away by government.

I could see in the faces in that room in New Hampshire that people were hearing something unexpected. A lot of us have heard the Founders evoked in speeches, of course, and we've certainly heard America hailed as the greatest country in the history of humanity. But something about marrying the promise of America with the gift of human potential seemed to strike a chord. I said what I fervently believe to be true: we are creatures of infinite potential blessed to live in a nation and at a time when very little is out of our reach. Our challenge is to unlock the potential of every American.

When I finished speaking, I took questions. A man in the back of the room stood up and simply said, "Amen." My luncheon companion approached me after the Q&A. "He stole my line," he said, referring to the pithy commenter. "The problem is, we don't think of ourselves as a nation of limitless possibility and potential anymore."

The comment stuck with me. I have traveled for almost a decade speaking to all kinds of people about all kinds of subjects. There is a sense of disquiet in our nation. It isn't partisan; it transcends politics. People fear we're losing something as a country. When the man at the New Hampshire Rotary Club said we are no longer a people who believe in limitless possibilities, I knew what it is we are losing. We are losing the sense that each of us has the right and the capacity to live life fully and on our own terms. And with that hope, the belief that has always defined the American Dream is being lost: that it doesn't matter what you look like or what your last name is. It is your gifts, your grit, and your potential that define your future. Today when we look to the future, instead of unlimited potential for all, we increasingly see shrunken, stilted lives defined by limitations, not possibilities.

I thought of the out-of-work men in Mendota. Politicians in a faraway capital had taken away their ability to live lives of dignity and purpose. I thought about the woman I met in South Carolina who dreamed of opening her own hair salon. But when she learned she had to claw her way through more than a year's worth of applying for licenses and regulations, her future was no longer limitless. She never opened her hair salon. And I thought of all the parents I've known. Every parent raising a child is struggling to unlock that child's potential. A good education is the indispensable support for them. But whether it's through the greed of a union boss or the cowardice of politicians, too many parents aren't getting that support, and too many children aren't realizing their potential. Their lives will be defined by a struggle just to make ends meet, not by a quest to achieve their dreams.

I thought of a statement by the president of the teachers union in Chicago the year the union struck against Mayor Rahm Emanuel. The issue was teacher accountability in the classroom. The president of the union said this: "We cannot be held accountable for the performance of children in our classrooms, because too many of them come from poor and broken families." What was she saying? In essence, that if you are poor or come from disadvantaged circumstances, you lack the potential to learn. Such a statement is an outrage and should be an affront to every American.

I know the power of human potential—I've felt it in my own life, and I've seen it countless times in others. It reveals itself in a challenge, in the unexpected, in the obstacle in your path that seems insurmountable.

I've come to know that every problem we face, every opportunity we have, can be solved by tapping the human potential possessed by *every* person. I've seen women in Africa use $150 loans to transform their lives and their families' lives. That's the power of human potential. If it can work in the poorest nations in the world, it can work in the richest nation on earth.

■ ■ ■

What unlocks human potential? Someone taking a chance on you. Someone giving you a helping hand. Free markets. An education. A job. And freedom.

Between President Obama telling business owners "you didn't build that" and Hillary Clinton assuring us that businesses don't create jobs, the American people could be forgiven for thinking that government unlocks human potential. The truth is quite the opposite. But President Obama and Secretary Clinton are right in this respect: no one succeeds on their own. Everyone at some point needs someone to encourage the potential that lies within. And every one of us, at one point or another, has needed a helping hand.

Government plays a role only insofar as it makes good on the Founders' commitment to every American's right to realize their God-given gifts. If you look at history, you see that human flourishing exploded beginning about the time two things first appeared: the new American republic and free market capitalism. If you plot the history of human prosperity going back over a thousand years, what you see is a flat line hovering just above zero until the late eighteenth century; then the line turns upward, and it hasn't turned back. Over the past forty years, as countries like China and India have adopted more pro-market policies, the number of people living in the most desperate poverty—existing on less than a dollar a day—has decreased by 80 percent.

Free markets unleash human potential. Free markets give men and women the opportunity to be entrepreneurs. Entrepreneurship exists when people have the opportunity to imagine something new, to take a risk, and to build it. The African women I've worked with who change their lives with $150 loans are entrepreneurs. In this country most entrepreneurs aren't found in Fortune 500 companies but in small businesses. It's the dry cleaners, the nail shops, the coffee shops, and the taquerias that are created by entrepreneurs, and it's these small businesses that create two thirds of our new jobs and employ half of all Americans. Small business entrepreneurs have created the greatest economic engine in the history of the world: the American economy.

Training and education also unlock human potential. When people have the tools and the confidence, they can dream bigger and utilize more of their gifts. Americans aren't poor because they lack potential. They are poor because they lack the tools and the opportunity to fulfill their potential. Education is an economic issue, and it is a life-defining issue. Students trapped in failing schools are much more likely to depend on public assistance as adults; they are much more likely to fail to achieve their potential.

A job unlocks human potential. When young people ask me what it takes to get ahead, I tell them to get a job, any job, because there is dignity in all work. When someone has a job, they not only have a sense of purpose, they learn the habits and skills necessary to get a better job. When politicians fail to emphasize jobs and work, they aren't being compassionate. They are wasting human potential.

Finally, freedom unlocks human potential: the freedom to find your own way and your own gifts; the freedom to make your own mistakes; the freedom to dream your own dreams.

What crushes human ambition and innovation? Among other things, powerful, unaccountable organizations dedicated to making sure nobody rocks the boat. In a word, bureaucracies. Dealing with bureaucracies saps our power, our passion, and our confidence. But don't just take my word for it. Ask the Desert Storm vet who walks into a waiting room filled with three hundred people at the Veterans Administration. Ask yourself how empowered you feel every time you go through TSA screening at the airport.

It's not that people inside a bureaucracy are bad. It's

that they quickly learn to keep their heads down, to not use their judgment, and certainly never take risks. The hallmark of bureaucracy is to avoid making tough choices by sending them up the chain. The people the bureaucracies were intended to serve come to be viewed more as hindrances than customers. They get in the way of the rules and processes that govern the bureaucracy. So the bureaucracy forces the people to bend to its needs rather than adapting to the needs of the people.

Contrast these huge, unaccountable, inefficient, and inflexible bureaucracies with a charity I work with called Good360, where I serve as chairman of the board. Good360 takes excess or obsolete inventory from companies and, through technology and our logistics and distribution expertise, matches that inventory to the needs of people served by over forty thousand charities in the United States. In a sense, we are like the eBay of the charitable world: we use technology to match charities on the ground with business inventory that would otherwise end up in a landfill or be destroyed for scrap. At Good360 about thirty people have matched and delivered over seven billion dollars' worth of goods, such as clothing, mattresses, books, computers, diapers, personal care products, and toys—everything but food and medicine—to people in need in America and around the world. A good example is the work we did in 2014, responding to the Ebola crisis. The charities in West Africa battling Ebola didn't necessarily need money. They needed rubber gloves, cleaning supplies, bottled water, and, tragically, body bags. These charities also asked for toys to comfort children who were isolated in quarantine, perhaps with a dying relative or dying themselves. In such dark, desperate circumstances, a cuddly toy can be hugged by a child or left to rot in a landfill.

Good360 is consistently named one of the top ten most efficient charities by *Forbes* magazine. And a small number of people at Good360 continue to innovate. Last year we developed technology called Disaster Recovery360. In essence, this is a portal that connects charities and first responders to the items they most need in the critical days and weeks following a disaster.

Whenever disaster strikes, whether it's Hurricane Katrina, the earthquake in Haiti, or Superstorm Sandy, Americans respond with generosity. Unfortunately, the vast majority of donations flow into a disaster area within six weeks of the event. Although these items are always appreciated, they are not always what is needed or can be used at the time. Sadly, 60 percent of all items generously donated after a disaster end up in landfill because they are the wrong goods at the wrong time.

In fact, during Superstorm Sandy the National Guard called on people to stop sending donations—they were literally clogging the streets and impeding disaster recovery efforts.

This is a huge waste, awful for our environment, disappointing to those who want to help, and devastating to those who need help. Good360's technology, which has been embraced by the Federal Emergency Management Agency (FEMA) and supported by corporate and foundation partners, allows charities and first responders on the ground to identify what, where, and when they need something, and then connects those needs with individuals and companies willing to fulfill them. And because the average community requires three years to recover from a disaster, we stay in a community and keep connecting people on the ground with those who are willing to help, long after the national media have moved on.

In short, just a few dozen people at Good360 have been able to achieve more than organizations ten times our size. We use technology effectively, and our great team, led by CEO Cindy Halberlin, has created a culture that encourages what bureaucracy stifles: accountability, innovation, entrepreneurialism, and the pursuit of excellence and impact.

Bureaucracies are almost always created to serve a need—to actually get something done—but over time they all have this characteristic: they become inwardly focused. They forget who they are there to serve and become dedicated to self-preservation. Sound familiar? It should. Washington, D.C., is composed of vast, unaccountable bureaucracies that are getting bigger every day. They've forgotten that they're there to serve the people and are interested only in their own power and survival. A good example is the Veterans Administration. It was created to serve our former warriors, particularly our wounded ones. Now it has been corrupted to serve only itself.

Bureaucracies crush human potential, but they do not do so equally. I know firsthand that the rules and regulations churned out by bureaucracies like the EPA and the IRS are relatively easy for big businesses to handle. Big corporations have the lawyers and the accountants to cut through the red tape. It's the small businesses whose potential is crushed. They can't afford to jump through all the hoops that bureaucracy creates, and that suits big business just fine. More regulations and more complex taxes mean less competition for them. One of the greatest fictions ever peddled by politicians is that big government is necessary to fight big business. In fact, the opposite is true. Big business and big government are mutually reinforcing. They need each other, and they know it. There's a reason why six of the wealthiest counties in America are directly adjacent to Washington, D.C. Big business pays big money for lobbyists to influence big government.

Bureaucracies and crony capitalism crush potential in America. The greatest lever for unlocking it is leadership. When I started out in my career in business, I used to think that leadership was measured in fancy titles, power, and corner offices. The men who had these things (and they were almost uniformly men) were the leaders, or so I thought. But I've learned since then that I was wrong. There are lots of people who have big power, big titles, and big offices who do not lead. We have a lot of these people in Washington right now. One has not only a big office, but an oval office.

True leadership is about seeing a different future and changing the order of things to achieve that future. The leader's job is not to be imprisoned by the conventional wisdom but to be out in front of it. As Margaret Thatcher said, you can't lead from the middle of a crowd. Leaders see things that others don't yet see, which is why they are frequently criticized in their time. Great leaders see great futures and lead the rest of us toward them.

The highest calling of leadership is to unlock the potential of others. I learned this early, when I was that young college graduate working as a secretary in that little, nine-person real estate firm. I had no big dreams; I was just trying to make a living. Then one day two men in that office came to my desk and said, "You know, Carly, we've been watching you. We think you have potential. We think you could do more than be a secretary. Do you want to know what we do?" That was my introduction to the world of business and the first step I took in fulfilling my potential. Theirs was an act of leadership.

For the parent, the small businessperson, or the out-of-work single mom, a leader is usually someone who takes a chance on them, just like those two men in that nine-person real estate firm did for me. To take a chance on someone is to empower them with tools and opportunity and then setting them free to go as far as they can go. All of us can go further than we think we can. I know this from hard experience. We all have more potential in us than we realize.

For the entrepreneur, leadership is envisioning a successful business and making it happen by unlocking the potential of employees. In 2014 I met such a leader in New Hampshire. Norm Carlson started building devices in his garage in 1996 to measure things like heat, humidity, speed, and pressure. He spent years marketing his products alone, sleeping in his car and shaving in his rearview mirror. Today he owns and operates MadgeTech in Warner, New Hampshire. He has fifty-four employees who design, manufacture, and produce products right there in New Hampshire and ship them all over the world. It's a MadgeTech sensor, for example, that monitors the Sistine Chapel in Rome to protect the priceless frescoes that adorn the walls and ceiling. Norm Carlson is a leader. And his leadership has unlocked the potential of his employees and his community.

Experience has also taught me that when we fail to achieve our potential, the easiest—and the most counterproductive—thing in the world is to look for someone to blame. The men and women who call themselves our leaders spend an awful lot of time pointing fingers and coming up with excuses.

There is a look in a person's eyes when they surprise themselves with how much they can achieve. It is the opposite of that flat, hollow look I saw in Lori's eyes and in the eyes of the men in Mendota. It is the look of hope. It lights people up from the inside. I've seen it countless times in the eyes of colleagues who have come together behind a common goal and achieved it. I've seen it in the eyes of young mothers in developing countries who have built new futures for themselves and their families as a result of the simple act of being loaned an amount less than the cost of a monthly cell phone plan.

For me, that look—of hope, of promise, of potential fulfilled—is fuel.

CHAPTER 2

A Soul Intact

FRANK REMEMBERS THE CALL BETTER THAN I do. He was exercising on his stationary bike, and I was upstairs asleep. It was President George W. Bush. He asked Frank if I was home. "Do you think I can talk to her?" Frank woke me up. "The president's on the phone," he said. It was February 10, 2005. The day before, I had been fired as the CEO of Hewlett-Packard.

There was an interesting duality to the days following my ouster from HP after six transformative years. On the one hand, the press coverage was ugly, and it was personal. I had done a difficult job in a difficult time in the technology industry. History would reveal that the changes I made alongside the extraordinary men and women of HP positioned the company to thrive in the years following my ouster. We had doubled the company's revenues to ninety billion dollars; accelerated the growth rate from 2 percent to 9 percent; quadrupled cash flow; gone from market laggard to market leader in every category; created jobs in America and around the world; and more than tripled our rate of innovation to eleven patents a day.

These facts were mostly overlooked in the press coverage. Some stories focused on the recent decline in the stock price, most ignoring that many other large-cap tech stocks like Cisco and Oracle were down about the same amount in that rocky, boom and bust period following the collapse of the dot-com bubble and the September 11 attacks. In fairness to the coverage, many companies avoid transformation and focus instead on short-term, quarterly earnings. The stock market is fickle and unforgiving— especially considering that the average holding period of stock has fallen to less than ninety days. My mandate at HP was to do the heavy lifting necessary to position the company for long-term success amid a rapidly changing industry. We did so, and the impact of that work revealed itself over the next several years, even if it wasn't reflected in that quarter's stock price.

There was a lot of both veiled and not-so-veiled sexist criticism of my leadership style. Instead of focusing on my record with the company—whether it was considered one of failure or success—so much of the coverage focused on me. Terms like "imperious witch" were thrown around—only the word used wasn't "witch," it just rhymed with it. I didn't read most of it. I had learned that lesson long ago from Oprah Winfrey. She had warned me not to believe my press coverage. If I believed the good stuff, she said, I had to believe the bad stuff. Poor Frank read it all, and it cut him like a knife.

On the other hand, in stark contrast to the public coverage of my leave-taking from HP were the private messages I received, including that call from President Bush. I had been helpful to him in an advisory capacity, and he wondered whether I was prepared to accept a job in his administration. Thousands of e-mails poured in, many from Hewlett-Packard employees. Frank and I spent hours reading them. With few exceptions, they expressed sympathy for me, anger at how I had been treated, and support for the work I had done.

I also heard from other leaders in the technology industry. One of the calls I remember with particular fondness came from Steve Jobs. We had become friends during my time in Silicon Valley. On the phone, Steve was very kind and generous. In other words, he was outraged. "They will regret this," he said. But more important than his supportive outrage was the advice he gave me.

"Carly, don't do anything for six months," he said. "People will inundate you with offers, and your instinct will be to jump back in. Don't. Just let it settle for six months." I took Steve's advice to heart.

I was disappointed at the behavior of Hewlett-Packard board members I thought I knew. I had behaved in what I believed was a principled fashion when confronted with the knowledge that a few members were leaking confidential boardroom conversations to the media. Fearing for their positions, they behaved in an unprincipled fashion and ousted me from mine.

It had been a time of testing. I had been at George W. Bush's inauguration when I got a phone call from a press person at HP saying there would be a front-page story the next day detailing confidential conversations our board had been engaged in at a recent meeting. I quickly arranged for an emergency phone call with the board. Frank later told me he had never seen me so angry. I told the board members about the pending story. The situation was very serious. The code of conduct had been violated. If the situation couldn't be corrected, I could not remain chairman. "Is there anyone who wants to say anything?" I asked. There was silence on the line. One of the members suggested that they all resign and I could reappoint those I chose as trustworthy. Believing that people I had worked with for years would ultimately behave honorably, I did not take that path. I should have.

Board members continued to deny that they were the leakers. I asked our outside counsel to conduct a series of interviews with each board member, hoping that individuals would come clean about their behavior. I knew who was leaking our conversations. However, it was more important that they acknowledge it to repair the serious breach of trust with every other board member. When outside counsel reported its findings to the board in a telephonic conference, I was attending the World Economic Forum in Davos, Switzerland. At 12:30 a.m. Davos time, I listened with dismay in my hotel room as the offending board members were neither candid nor forthcoming. Two weeks later I was fired.

The truth is, I could have prevented my dismissal, but I was neither prepared to sacrifice my principles nor subject the company to a prolonged period of conflict that would have continued to play out on front pages around the world. As chairman of the board, I had a vote on every matter before the board, including my position as chairman and CEO. I chose not to exercise that right. In the end, I lost the final vote on my position by a single vote. Had I exercised my right to vote, I could have tied up the board for months and kept my job. I had concluded, however, that it wasn't in the interests of HP to have an ongoing boardroom fight. Nor was it in my interest. My colleagues weren't prepared to deal with the board members who were leaking confidential information in a way that I thought appropriate. The fact that these same board members were fired a year later for conduct unbecoming a board member is testimony, I believe, to the legitimacy of the actions I had both proposed and taken. Still, prolonging the conflict would have damaged the company at a delicate time. So I accepted my dismissal without a fight.

Despite my disappointment with how my tenure had ended, my overriding emotion after leaving HP was a sense of freedom. It's a long climb from secretary to CEO. My days as CEO were unrelenting. For the first time in a long time, I felt like I could do whatever I wanted. The sense of liberation reminded me of how I felt the day I quit law school. I hated law school, despite my father's obvious enthusiasm for wanting another lawyer in the family. Then one day while taking a shower, I realized—in a revelation that felt like a bolt from heaven—my life was my own; I could do what I wanted with it. I got dressed, walked downstairs, and told my mom and dad, "I quit."

Although I had loved every minute while serving as the chief executive of HP, I felt that same sense of liberation in those months that followed my departure. And this time, I had the time and the means to truly do whatever I wanted. I didn't want to lose that feeling, so I took Steve's advice and savored the excitement of the possibilities that lay ahead. I was offered interesting opportunities to serve on corporate and nonprofit boards, but I turned them down. I had no desire to go back into a boardroom just yet. And I didn't want to be a CEO—I had had enough of quarterly earnings for a while.

Frank and I quickly decided to get away. I couldn't go anywhere in California without being recognized, and it made me feel self-conscious. Of course, the same thing turned out to be true in Hawaii, where we spent a week.

People would come up to me and express their support. I truly appreciated their kindness, but it was awkward.

Another important decision I faced after leaving HP was when and how I was going to speak publicly about my experience. This was a pivotal moment, and one that I had thought about for some time. When I was forced out at Hewlett-Packard, the board asked me to put out a statement describing my departure as mutually agreed upon by the board and me because we had achieved our agreed objectives. I refused. It would have been false. I had been fired. And I wasn't going to live a lie for the rest of my life. My sincere belief then, as now, is that given enough time and enough information, people will figure things out. In the end, the truth will always come out. The press coverage had raged for months, and I gave not a single interview or speech. I knew there would come a time when I would set the record straight.

Before I left Hewlett-Packard there were a number of speaking engagements on my calendar for the spring of 2005. I canceled most of them, but there was one I paused over. It was an invitation to give the commencement address at North Carolina A&T, a historically black college in Greensboro. I was familiar with the school. North Carolina A&T graduates more African American students into the technology professions—including more African American women who go into careers in science, math, and technology—than any other school. Hewlett-Packard did quite a bit of hiring among its graduates.

Giving the commencement speech at such a school interested me because I knew many in the audience had to overcome significant obstacles to get into the school and would face more once they got out. Throughout my experiences I have come to know that people who have learned to overcome much can achieve more than people who've never been tested. So I called the school and asked whether they still wanted me to come. "Yes," they said. I began writing a speech that would speak candidly—and, I hoped, helpfully—about overcoming obstacles.

Like all speeches should, mine began with some humor. I addressed the graduates as "my fellow job seekers." I told them about how, after the news of my departure from HP broke, I called the school and asked whether they wanted to rescind their invitation. The chancellor told me no. If anything, he said, I had more in common with the graduates now than before.

"And he's right," I said. "After all, I've been working on my resume. I've been lining up my references. I bought a new interview suit. If there are any recruiters here, I'll be free around eleven."

For the first time, I told the graduates the stories I would later relate in *Tough Choices*. I talked about the obstacles and prejudgments I had encountered working my way up in the corporate world. I told them about being referred to as "our token bimbo" by my boss, and sitting through an uncomfortable luncheon meeting in a strip club called, ironically, The Board Room. My male colleagues had decided to meet a client there—and then basically dared me to attend. I knew the students at North Carolina A&T had their own stories—many of which would make mine seem minor in comparison. I encouraged them to continue to meet challenges head on.

"Never," I said, "sell your soul. What I mean by not selling your soul is don't be someone you're not, don't be less than you are, don't give up what you believe, because whatever the consequences that may seem scary or bad—whatever the consequences of staying true to yourself are—they are much better than the consequences of selling your soul."

The Greensboro Coliseum was filled to capacity for the graduation ceremony. Commencement speeches are always tall orders—the students are usually too eager to celebrate to have much time to listen to a speaker drone on. I was relieved to find the audience receptive, even eager. And then I got to the words that I had been waiting four months to say.

"Many people have asked me how I feel now that I've lost my job," I told the graduates. "The truth is, I'm proud of the life I've lived so far, and though I've made my share of mistakes, I have no regrets. The worst thing I could have imagined happened. I lost my job in the most public way possible, and the press had a field day with it all over the world. And guess what? I'm still here."

The coliseum erupted in cheers as the audience leapt

to their feet. I don't flatter myself to think that the response was because these young people were so invested in my story. I told a very human story that day, one to which I think we all aspire: to come through the storm with our dignity intact. To do more than survive—to thrive—because whatever judgments are hurled at you from the outside, whatever public indignities you endure, inside you are confident in your own integrity.

"I am at peace and my soul is intact," I said, previewing the words I would later write in my book. "I could have given it away and the story would be different. But I heard the word of Scripture in my head: 'What benefit will it be to you if you gain the whole world but lose your soul?'"

■ ■ ■

Not long after the North Carolina A&T speech, Adrian Zackheim of Portfolio / Penguin Publishing contacted me about writing a book. He wrote me a very convincing letter, but I wasn't sure. Frank and I were enjoying our freedom. We rented a van and drove across the country. We had fun. We bought an apartment to be closer to our family. Both Lori and Tracy were living in Virginia. Tracy had given us two granddaughters, Kara and Morgan. We adored them completely and their mother, our daughter, is a constant source of deep joy and great pride.

As the summer of 2005 went on, I still wasn't sure about writing a book. The North Carolina A&T speech was the most personal speech I had ever given. I poured a great deal of myself into it and was pleased with how it had been received. People asked me all the time why I didn't want the catharsis that supposedly comes with writing a book. In truth, I felt that I had already achieved it. I was able to look back on what had happened at HP with a great deal of dispassion, as if I were in the audience watching myself on stage in a play. I wasn't sure whether I wanted to revisit all the scenes of triumph and betrayal in my story. I had achieved a comfortable distance.

It wasn't until September that I truly decided to write a book. The first thing I needed to do was write an outline. I worked methodically, taking two and a half months to produce a first draft. The book I wanted to write was a view of the business world, focusing on the people who form it. For me, business is a story about people—what they are capable of when supported and challenged; what they can envision and create—which is why I like the business world. The outline I wrote was pretty wonky, more of a management how-to book than a memoir. Adrian encouraged me to go back to the drawing board and tell more of my own story.

I had succeeded in the business world by producing results, not by telling my story. Still, I underestimated, I am sure, how important it is for people to know who their leader is. A person's character isn't just revealed by actions in the present but by the actions of a lifetime. And those actions eventually accumulate to become a story.

Once Adrian convinced me that the book must feature more of my personal story, I knew it was something I had to write myself. This made Adrian nervous. He wanted me to work with a collaborator, but ultimately I prevailed. Writing the book was a challenging—but ultimately very rewarding—process. I worked at my home in Silicon Valley, in the carriage house, where I had set up an office. I had a window that looked out on some oak trees. I set a goal for myself of writing a chapter a day. I would write ten to twelve hours a day. Every night Frank would read the day's product as it came off the printer. Working at this clip, I began writing the manuscript in December 2005, went through three drafts, and finished in March 2006.

I had spent a lifetime taking my energy from people, so the solitary work of writing a book was something different. Every morning I felt as though I were lowering myself down into a dark cave. It was difficult getting there, but once I was down, it was exhilarating. It felt roomy and well lit and interesting. All my fears of reliving the painful parts of my story were unfounded. It turns out, when you refuse to compromise yourself, explaining yourself isn't difficult. And so the story flowed out of me. Yes, I had been fired from HP, but in the most important sense, I had departed on my own terms. I knew there would be consequences to my actions, but I didn't believe I had any choice.

I honestly enjoyed writing *Tough Choices*, but it was the reception the book received when it was released in September 2006 that was most heartening. I followed Oprah's advice and didn't take the reviews in the press too seriously. On my book tour it was ordinary people who came up to me and told me how much they appreciated my story and how it had inspired them. It is always people who save me, lift me, and give me joy. People can't relate to a story of a steady upward trajectory, free of any missteps or setbacks. Everyone has ups and downs, and when you share them honestly, people appreciate it. To this very day I receive heartfelt messages from people all over the world thanking me for writing *Tough Choices*. Men and women still approach me, book in hand, to ask for my autograph. Every one of those messages and encounters is a blessing to me.

In particular, young women came up to me to thank me for writing the book. It was depressing how many young women told me they had had the same kind of experiences with sexist male colleagues that I wrote about. It reminded me that although we've come a long way, we haven't come far enough. Women remain an underutilized resource in business, in politics, and in communities. Women are still too often treated with disrespect and marginalized. The burden of poverty falls most heavily on women and their children. Even more tragically, women and girls are too often the victims of domestic abuse, sexual assault, sexual slavery, and rape.

Sadly, the feminist movement has become politicized and captured by a left-wing agenda. My definition of feminism is that every woman has the chance to choose her own life—whether she chooses to homeschool her children or start a business. Modern-day feminism has transformed itself from being a movement that sought to treat women as equals with men to an orthodoxy that seeks to portray all men as the enemy and women as requiring the constant assistance of government. I believe we will have arrived—men and women together—when we realize that women represent half the human potential of our nation and of the world. If we want better lives and a better world, we must fully engage the God-given gifts of every woman and every man. Girls and boys should be able to look forward to their future with optimism and confidence rather than fear and deprivation.

■ ■ ■

In a moment of cosmic symmetry, *Tough Choices* came out just as news broke that the California attorney general's office was investigating the Hewlett-Packard board. It seems HP had hired private investigators to pose as board members, some of whom were still leaking, in order to obtain board members' and journalists' private phone records. The technique, known as pretexting, was supposedly used to try to determine which board members were leaking the confidential details of HP board meetings. HP acknowledged hiring an outside firm to investigate the leaks earlier in the year, but company executives denied knowing that the investigators engaged in pretexting or any other illegal practices to identify the leakers.

Congress jumped on the scandal and decided to hold hearings. I remember watching hours of testimony by HP executives on CNBC, which carried the hearings live. I watched in disbelief as my former general counsel—along with several other witnesses—invoked the Fifth Amendment and refused to testify. Into this media firestorm, my book was released. I was inundated with questions about pretexting and the congressional hearings. Some asked me whether I was responsible for ordering the pretexting as CEO. In fact, I had been a victim of it.

My calls had been monitored without my knowledge after I left Hewlett-Packard. Still, it was a sad spectacle to see former colleagues and my successors the subject of congressional oversight hearings. The betrayal and dysfunction that had led to my departure had not only continued but also deepened.

For five years following my departure, HP performed extremely well. All of the previous years' hard work came to fruition. Unfortunately, that five-year period of leadership was squandered when management focused on short-term earnings and failed to invest sufficiently in the lifeblood of a technology company: innovation. The hard truth about leadership and success is that it can never be taken for granted. It must always be invested in. When companies—or countries for that matter—begin to rest on their laurels and take comfort in their past triumphs or their present performance, the future begins to dim just a bit. The past is not prologue to the future. The future must always be built.

As of this writing, HP is on its fourth CEO in less than a decade and its fifth chairman. The board has almost completely turned over, and the company is splitting in two. For me it is a reminder of the power a handful of people can wield to do tremendous harm.

■ ■ ■

The months after the publication of *Tough Choices* were full of opportunities for me to speak to Americans from all walks of life. And although I had acceded to my publisher's wishes and written a very personal book, I found myself at podiums across the country talking about my book as I had originally envisioned it: less as a story about me than a story about the people of the business world. Experience had taught me it is *people* who produce the products and profits of business, and if you don't understand people, you can't change what they do. Which is to say, you cannot lead.

Many of the technologists—the engineers and coders—I have worked with throughout my career consider the human element of the technology business as the "soft" side, less important than the work they do. As a CEO, I told audiences on my book tour, I saw people differently. The essence of leadership is seeing the possibilities of people. In this respect, leadership differs critically from management. Management is the production of acceptable results within known conditions and constraints. Leadership, in contrast, is about looking beyond the known, breaking through constraints, and changing the order of things.

Two things complicate a leader's ability to change an organization. The first is that people both crave change and fear change—they are both excited by and afraid of the unknown. Second, people who have power and influence want to keep their power and influence. The status quo advantages them, and they will use their power to protect the status quo. The result is that any organization, be it a company or a government, has a tendency toward complacency and stagnation. It resists leaders who attempt to change the order of things.

This was the situation I encountered when I came to Hewlett-Packard in 1999. HP had a rich and storied history of innovation in Silicon Valley. Much of that is thanks to a company credo developed by founders Bill Hewlett and Dave Packard. The "HP way" emphasized achievement, contribution, flexibility, and innovation.

Over the years, though, what had been a meritocracy at HP devolved into a bureaucracy. By the late 1990s, HP lagged behind in every market in which we competed, except printers, where we still led, but our profit margins had been cut in half—all this mediocre performance in the midst of a technology boom. People at the company stopped adhering to the "HP way" and started using it as an excuse not to innovate—as in, "We can't change X. That's not the HP way." What had been a positive, innovation-supporting culture became tired, bureaucratic convention.

My book was about how I set out to transform the culture at Hewlett-Packard to restore the company's proud history of innovation. It was the story of my efforts to envision a new future for HP and the very human resistance I encountered in doing so. In the course of going around the country talking about my book, I started to get asked questions about issues outside HP. I came to realize how much of what I had learned about leadership applied to many of the challenges the country as a whole was facing. Even before the recession began, for instance, American jobs were going overseas and American wages were stagnating. Both technology and globalization were affecting our economy. I said we needed to fight for every job. We could not take our past economic leadership for granted. We had to invest in our future by competing hard in every industry, by improving our education and job-training policies so that our children and our workers were prepared to fill twenty-first century jobs, and by changing our tax and regulatory climate so that we were the best place to do business in the world. All of these changes and investments would require leaders who understood that America could no longer afford to be complacent. In short, I said, we had to compete for jobs and prepare our workers to succeed in them.

It turned out there were many in government who thought my experience in transforming HP and working in the technology industry and the global economy were relevant to the challenges they faced. And so at that time I was asked to serve as the chairman of the External Advisory Board for the Central Intelligence Agency by then-CIA Director Michael Hayden; to serve on the Defense Business Board by its chairman, Michael Bayer, under Secretaries of Defense Rumsfeld and Gates; and on the Advisory Committee for Transformational Diplomacy, chaired by former Michigan governor John Engler under Secretary of State Condoleezza Rice.

Each of these fine secretaries realized they sat astride gigantic bureaucracies that would outlast their tenure. All feared that the challenges they faced were in many cases outstripping their institutions' ability to adequately respond and keep pace. They knew they were shackled by complexity and inertia. And all knew as well that they needed the experience and perspective of people from outside the bureaucracy to change it.

General Hayden asked the Advisory Board to focus on several key questions:

How should an agency that conducted its work in secret provide an appropriate level of transparency and accountability to the American public so that support was ensured—particularly for difficult missions and controversial actions? How should the agency's IT systems be transformed in an era when the agency must continue to encrypt and protect information while at the same time collaborate and share with other agencies? How should a sophisticated system cope with the reality that our enemies were using basic, ubiquitous technologies to organize and attack us? How should the recruitment of personnel change given the new realities of terrorism in the twenty-first century?

We debated how, why, and whether the bureaucratic process had corrupted the executive summary of the 2007 National Intelligence Estimate on Iran, which declared with "high confidence" that Iran had halted its nuclear weapons development in 2003 and had "moderate confidence" it had not resumed its efforts as of 2007. Finally, we discussed frequently and at length the creation of the Department of National Intelligence and the numerous, usually onerous, and not always productive requests for information, management directives, and budget imperatives that this new and powerful bureaucracy created for the CIA.

Secretary Rice asked the Advisory Committee for

Transformational Diplomacy to look at personnel recruitment, IT systems, and collaboration and coordination with other government agencies—particularly the Department of Defense (DOD). At the Defense Business Board, we examined the spaghettilike charts that depicted all the appropriations processes that were required to get any changes at the DOD approved. These processes virtually guaranteed that change was extremely difficult at best and impossible at worst—something Secretary Gates would later write about poignantly in *Duty*, his memoir. We debated the solutions to a vexing problem: how, in the middle of fighting two wars, when the needs of our brave men and women in uniform were desperate and too often unmet, could the DOD be spending so much more money on the bureaucracy at the Pentagon? This so-called tooth-to-tail ratio was as out of whack as it had ever been, despite heroic leadership effort to change it. We also undertook a specific project focused on how the business community could work more closely with both the Departments of State and Defense in furthering American objectives in hot spots around the world.

The work was fascinating and challenging. I was grateful to have an opportunity to serve with men and women whom I admired. The experience also reinforced my views that people are people wherever you find them, and, therefore, bureaucracy is bureaucracy, whether in business or government. Change is change and always extremely difficult—particularly when undertaken in vast organizations where turf wars abound and everyone has pet projects and sacred cows. Yet if change is not successfully pursued in our federal agencies, these bureaucratic leviathans will consume more and more money and produce fewer and fewer acceptable results. It is the nature of the beast.

I got involved in politics because I know that politicians and the policies they pursue affect all our lives in very real ways. We have all the human potential we need to solve every problem, heal every wound, and allow every American man, woman, and child to build a life of dignity and purpose. What we need are different policies and different leaders.

■ ■ ■

In the midst of my service in our defense and intelligence communities in the summer of 2007, Senator John McCain's staff told me the senator wanted to meet with me. I had known John since 2000, when I came to Capitol Hill to testify against Internet taxation. As chairman of the Commerce Committee, he agreed with me; we bonded over our shared desire to preserve the freedom to innovate on the Web. Now he was in the midst of a campaign for the Republican presidential nomination, and things were going badly. He was unhappy, and his performances showed it. Fund-raising was sluggish, and his advisers were riven with conflicts. Out of money, he was forced to lay off half his campaign staff. The national press had written him off as a contender.

I went to see him in his Senate office, and he asked me for help on the campaign. As much as I admired Senator McCain, I had to think about it. I had never endorsed a candidate before. As CEO, I always believed that I represented all the people in the company and shouldn't get involved in partisan politics. After reading his memoir, *Faith of My Fathers*, my belief in John's candidacy and my desire to learn more about life on the campaign trail got the better of me, and I agreed. Before long I was on the road with him.

I found myself a small part of a campaign that was genuinely on a shoestring in the summer of 2007. It was a bare-bones operation. The hotels were cheap, the entourage was small, and the senator carried his own bag. The first place we traveled together was to South Carolina. It was just Senator McCain, his press secretary, Brooke Buchanan, and me. When we were less than ten minutes away from the first stop, Brooke turned to me and said, "You're going to introduce him, okay?" I was surprised, but I managed to respond by saying, yes, of course I will introduce him, just give me the notes you've prepared. But there were no notes; there was nothing. "Just talk about yourself," Brooke said. So with seven minutes of warning, I got up in front of the crowd, said briefly who I was and why I admired John McCain.

Somehow it worked. I began to travel with him regularly.

As the summer wore on, the McCain campaign began to slowly engineer one of the great comebacks in presidential nomination campaign history. John quit trying to run as the inevitable establishment front-runner and returned to the scrappy challenger role he was more comfortable in. And pretty soon, the crummy rental car we had been traveling in became a bus. The media called off the death watch. Fund-raising picked up, and the crowds at events got bigger. After John secured the GOP nomination in March 2008, my role in the campaign became more formal. I spoke to groups of women. I traveled with John to talk about economic issues. I even got the Straight Talk Express for a trip through Ohio and Pennsylvania to speak about the necessity of creating jobs and growing the economy.

On August 27, two days before the campaign announced the pick, John called me and told me that he'd chosen Alaska governor Sarah Palin as his running mate. He had a request. "She's going to need help, Carly," he said. He wanted me to help her get up to speed on the economic issues facing the country. The subprime mortgage crisis had been building for months. Bear Stearns had been bailed out in March. Lehman Brothers would fall in a matter of weeks. I told Senator McCain I would be glad to help her.

I thought the pick of Governor Palin as Senator McCain's running mate was different—but in a good way.

She was an unknown quantity to me, but her candidacy added needed excitement and energy to the race. I remember sitting next to Henry Kissinger at the Republican National Convention in St. Paul as Governor Palin gave her famous speech on the third night of the convention. Like a lot of people in the arena, Henry didn't know what to expect. But about six minutes into the speech, he started elbowing me in the ribs and exclaiming, "She's really good! Maybe this is going to work!" We all thought that.

The reaction of many Democrats and much of the mainstream media, however, was harsh, immediate, and thoroughly sexist. Before Governor Palin even had the chance to address the convention, I stood at a press conference with other female McCain supporters, such as Tennessee representative Marsha Blackburn and former Massachusetts governor Jane Swift, and condemned the attacks on Palin—as well as similar attacks on Hillary Clinton—as sexist. My argument wasn't that it was sexist to question Governor Palin's qualifications to be vice president. What was sexist was holding her to a different standard than a man, like Barack Obama.

"I think it's very legitimate to have a debate about relevant experience," I told Charlie Rose the night of her speech. "But honestly I think it is dismissive of a woman to say that a man who has been a one-time, one-term U.S. senator and has never made an executive decision in his life has more experience to be president of the United States than a woman who has made many executive decisions in her life is qualified to be vice president of the United States."

It would not be the last time I would be called on to defend Governor Palin. I was glad to do it. The attacks on her—which ranged from rumors that she had faked her pregnancy to suggestions that she was a Nazi sympathizer—were beyond the pale. I never did get the chance to fulfill Senator McCain's request to brief her on the economic challenges facing the country, although I made numerous requests to meet with her during the campaign. To this day I have never met her.

■ ■ ■

When the dominoes inevitably began to fall during those last months of the campaign, panic set in. Wall Street bankers, Treasury officials—all the players in the drama—were stressed and sleep deprived. Treasury Secretary Hank Paulson had brought all the heads of the Wall Street firms to Washington, got them into a room, and pushed a piece of paper in front of them. The message was clear: you will sign this, and you will take a government bailout. As Congress debated the $700 billion bailout, McCain suspended his campaign and flew to Washington. Although I thought this was a bad idea, I wasn't consulted, and I knew there were many who were urging McCain to take dramatic action.

In the end, the House voted down the bill on October

29. Later, a revised version was passed and signed by President Bush that became known as TARP, or the Troubled Assets Relief Program. In the years since, we've seen yet another case of the unintended consequences of government intervention and overcorrection. We gave the big banks the money they needed to survive. Fannie and Freddie—which had created the market for risky mortgages to begin with at the behest of politicians who claimed that home ownership is a necessary part of the American Dream—escaped unscathed. Another massive piece of legislation, the Dodd-Frank Act, accompanied by thousands of pages of additional regulation, was passed to "protect" the little guy and ensure appropriate regulatory oversight of the big, bad Wall Street banks. The myriad regulatory agencies had failed in their oversight duties before the financial crisis, but somehow the creation of yet another system of oversight and more regulation was going to fix the problem. Congress tightened the capital requirements for lenders even as they asked banks to lend. The result of all this has been a massive consolidation. Ten banks too big to fail have become five banks too big to fail. If you are JPMorgan Chase or Goldman Sachs, you are in a better competitive situation than you were ten years ago. And if you are a large company, you can get all kinds of credit.

Hurt in this process? Smaller community banks that had nothing to do with exotic financial instruments like collateralized debt obligations (CDOs). These banks struggle to compete and aren't making loans to the families and family-owned businesses they've traditionally supported. Also hurt in this process? Small businesses that can't get credit; families whose home values plummeted through no fault of their own; and the hardworking, honest Americans who want credit but now can't get it because the standards have become too onerous. Crony capitalism rears its ugly head once again. The same pattern played out in the bailout of General Motors. A big company and all its union jobs were saved. Meanwhile, the auto dealerships, repair shops, and suppliers out on Main Street that had served General Motors were wiped out. In fact, more jobs were lost in our communities than all the union jobs saved. And no one in Washington seemed to take any notice at all.

There are those who have said that any candidate of the incumbent president's party running in the midst of the greatest financial crisis since the Great Depression would have lost the election. Maybe they're right. I only know that although I didn't agree with everything John McCain said or did, he is one of the most honorable men I have ever known. However, I couldn't help him in those final weeks of the election. I was removed as a surrogate.

In an interview on a St. Louis radio station, I had been asked if Governor Palin had the experience to run Hewlett-Packard. My first mistake was to answer the question—Sarah Palin was running for vice president, not CEO. Still, I foolishly answered with the truth. No, I said, I didn't think she could. Not because she didn't have the potential—after all, I had started as a secretary—but because she didn't have the requisite training or experience. Later, when asked to clarify, I said that neither John McCain nor Barack Obama nor Joe Biden could run HP either. But then again, I said, I couldn't fly a fighter jet like John McCain could. There are some jobs that require a level of technical expertise and particular experience. The CEO job is such a job, just as being a fighter pilot is such a job. And while being president or vice president of the United States requires relevant experience, our nation was intended to be a citizen government. Many experiences qualify. What was important was whether John McCain or Barack Obama was more qualified to be president of the United States. And on that question, there was no doubt.

I had taken on the challenge of the campaign because I believed in John McCain and I wanted to learn. Suffice it to say, I learned a painful and important lesson. Even a "Washington gaffe"—that is, a misstatement that is impolitic but nonetheless true—has consequences. I had enjoyed my time on the campaign trail speaking for Senator McCain. Now I was beginning to think perhaps it was best for me to speak for myself.

■　■　■

Just before the holidays in 2008 I was approached by California Republican committeeman Shawn Steel about running for the U.S. Senate. Duf Sundheim, who was running a group tasked with recruiting GOP candidates, also contacted me. Barbara Boxer was up for reelection in 2010, and they wanted to know if I was interested in challenging her.

Boxer had first come to Washington in 1982, when Ronald Reagan's presidency was young and no one had ever heard of a cell phone, much less the Internet. She had been in the Senate for eighteen years and was gunning for six more. She had never been very popular, with approval ratings that perennially hovered at less than 50 percent. Despite that, the GOP had never been able to field a candidate who could unseat her. This year was going to be different, Steel and Sundheim said. The political climate was ripe for someone who would stand in contrast to Boxer's dogmatic liberalism.

I was flattered that they would think of me, and I was intrigued but wary. I have never been someone who backs down from a challenge. I have, in fact, found that challenging myself is the best way to learn and grow. Nor am I someone who takes on things that are unachievable; I don't tilt at windmills. This was new territory for me, and Boxer was a seasoned politician. I was, as the press never ceased to remind me, a novice in the world of politics.

There was something about that word, "novice," when used in the political context, that didn't sit well with me. For most of the history of this republic, our elected officials moved in and out of private life and public service. Most of our political leaders, in other words, were novices. From the time of our founding and for 150 years, we regarded the citizen legislator—the person who brings the perspective and experience of ordinary life to Washington, D.C.—as a good thing. The professional politician is a modern invention and not an improvement. Barbara Boxer had known nothing but Washington for almost thirty years. Why, I wondered, was being a novice not a point in my favor?

As for the data, they were mixed as to whether challenging Senator Boxer was a good move. A Field Poll released in February showed a California electorate evenly split on Boxer's reelection, with 43 percent in favor and 54 percent opposed.* If Senator Boxer was vulnerable, she clearly knew it and was preparing. No more than an hour after the *San Jose Mercury News* reported that I might be a candidate, Boxer sent out a fund-raising appeal warning of my candidacy.† At the beginning of 2009—still almost two years from the election—she had $4.6 million amassed in her campaign war chest, culled from the usual California liberal donors in Hollywood and Silicon Valley. There were also large donations from energy companies eager to curry favor with Senator Boxer as the chairman of the Environment and Public Works Committee. The Senate was

---

*Frank Davies, "Sen. Boxer, Looking over Shoulder at Fiorina, Has Raised $4.6 Million for Re-election," *San Jose Mercury News*, April 20, 2009.

† Ibid.

due to debate legislation designed to combat global warming—legislation that would be drafted in Chairman Boxer's committee. All the energy companies wanted to be at the table, not on the menu.

As I considered my decision, I knew that taking on Barbara Boxer meant taking on the Washington insiders and entrenched interests that had kept her in power for almost three decades. If I were to challenge her, I would also be challenging the culture of cronyism that she represented. This much I knew. What I did not yet know was that an even greater challenge lay right in front of me.

CHAPTER 3

Cancer

I WAS IN A BATHTUB IN MEXICO WHEN I FOUND the lump.

I had just taken up Pilates, and as anyone who has done the plank can attest, I was sore, especially under my arms. Sitting back in the hot bathtub at the end of a long day, I massaged my aching muscles. The lump was about the size of a dime, in the middle of my armpit. My immediate reaction was to pull back and think, "I didn't feel that." I felt again. It was definitely there. My next thought was "I'm not going to worry about this. I feel fine. I just had my mammogram. I'm on vacation!" So I pushed it to the back of my mind. Two days later, in the bathtub again, the lump was still there. I told

Frank I needed to see my doctor when we returned home.

I had my regular physical scheduled in two weeks, but I was concerned enough to call my doctor right away. She was sure it was nothing—she knew I'd had a clear mammogram—but told me to come in. In her office she felt the lump. "I don't think this is what you fear it is," she said. "But just to be sure, let's get it biopsied." She was very reassuring. The biopsy was quick and relatively painless. Once again, I put it out of my mind.

My physical was on a Friday, February 20, 2009. As usual, I had a packed schedule. I was supposed to be at the doctor's office from 9 to 10 a.m. Then I had an interview on Bloomberg Television in downtown San Francisco. After that, Frank, my friend and colleague Deborah Bowker, and I were going to drive up to Sacramento for the California Republican Convention, where I was giving several speeches. With a busy day very much on my mind, I arrived at the doctor's office right on time. After the appointment, I would meet Frank and Deborah back at my house, where my bags were packed and ready to go.

Dr. Sarah Watson, who is normally very punctual, wasn't ready to see me at 9 a.m. I waited in an ill-fitting paper gown in a cold examining room until 9:15, and she still hadn't arrived. Nine-thirty came—no doctor. By 9:40 I was getting concerned. At 9:45 she walked into the room. Looking very pale, she sat down. She apologized and said she had been on the phone confirming some bad news. "You have cancer," she said. "We don't know what kind. We need to begin tests immediately."

I remember having this strange sensation of being both shocked and unsurprised. My grandmother had died of stomach cancer when my mother was just ten. My aunt had battled breast cancer. For my whole life, somewhere in the back of my mind, I had always thought I was going to get it too. Maybe we all have that dread. At that moment, in my doctor's office, I felt a wave of warm, pent-up fear wash over me. It had happened. I had cancer.

I felt light-headed, vaguely nauseated, and shaky. I willed myself to be calm. And I did what I have done my whole life when confronted by a new situation: I started asking questions. Because Dr. Watson had said they didn't know what kind of cancer I had, asking more questions about my diagnosis seemed like a waste of time. I concentrated on trying to be practical and analytical. I asked questions that seem obvious in retrospect, but at the time filled my need to learn as much as possible about the unknowns that now faced me. "Will I need chemotherapy?" I asked. "Yes," she said. "Will I need surgery?" "Yes." "How long will this go on?" "I don't know."

She immediately started listing the doctors I would need to see for different tests. As she went on, I knew I should be grateful for her knowledge and for the expertise of the other men and women she reeled off, one after another. And I was grateful. But my survival mechanism is to focus hard and concentrate on a task, and it kicked in. The task at hand was to stay on schedule. And it was already after 10 a.m.

As soon as she finished, I spoke up. "I hate to say this, but I have to leave in fifteen minutes, and I need a Pap smear before I go," I said. She looked a little taken aback, but she proceeded to give me the physical I was there to have. And as she worked, she gave me what I would come to understand was very good advice.

"Carly, one of the most important things you have to do is decide when you're going to share this news with anyone," she said. "Don't be surprised if people are very intrusive, very personal, and want to tell you their own personal stories. You have to know that you can say, 'Enough. I can't handle this.'"

She also told me that some people wouldn't be able to handle me as a cancer patient. These people would drift out of my life. Others would surprise me and be guardians and friends during the journey that was ahead.

Time would reveal how right she was. Once you tell someone—let alone the world—that you have cancer, everything changes. Conversation revolves around little else. Other people afflicted by the disease—either in themselves or a loved one—discover a kinship in you. Strangers tell you intimate stories and express sincere concern.

So much of it is heartwarming. When you are ill—or frightened, as I was—all of it is exhausting.

Before I left her office, my doctor gave me a second piece of advice. She handed me a prescription for a sleeping pill. "Make sure you get plenty of rest," she said. "This is going to be a long haul."

■ ■ ■

I had met Deborah Bowker in 1988 at the Massachusetts Institute of Technology (MIT). As a manager working my way up the ranks at AT&T, the company had sent me to MIT to earn a master of science in business administration. Deborah was one of the few other women at the Sloan School of Management, and we became the best of friends. We went our separate professional ways after that but always stayed close. After I left Hewlett-Packard in 2005, Deborah and I decided to become business partners. Our husbands thought it would ruin our friendship (it hasn't), but we formed Carly Fiorina Enterprises in 2007. That morning after my doctor's appointment, she was scheduled to accompany me to the Bloomberg interview and then drive with Frank and me to Sacramento. In the car on the way home from the doctor's office, I called her and gave her the news.

She was sitting in her car in front of my house waiting for me when she got the call. She was early, as usual. "What should I do?" I asked. I was worried about me, of course, but my immediate concern was for Frank. How would I tell him? Should we stick with our itinerary and go to the convention in Sacramento? All of the emotions that I had successfully kept bottled up in the doctor's office came rushing out. I asked Deborah once again, this time more urgently, "What do you think I should do?"

Maybe Deborah and I get along so well because we are so much alike. She was shocked at hearing the news. She told me she would do anything she could to help and support me. Then she got practical. "Carly, if you don't go to Sacramento, that's perfectly fine. No one would blame you," she said. "But just think about it. If you don't go, you and Frank are going to sit in the house all weekend and hold hands and be anxious. What good is that?"

As I made the short trip to my house, I thought about what she had said. Deborah was right. Nothing was going to happen until Monday, when the tests began. What point would there be for me—and Frank—to sit around the house and worry for forty-eight hours? When I got home, I asked Frank to sit down in the same living room in which the policemen would stand a year and a half later to tell us Lori had died. I told him that the lump was cancerous, but they didn't know what kind. I thought about Deborah waiting outside in her car and tried to steer the conversation toward the immediate decision we had to make: should we go to Sacramento or not?

Frank was initially against going. He was concerned that it would be too much for me. I pushed back. There was a lot of speculation that I was contemplating running for the Senate against three-term incumbent Barbara Boxer. I was, in fact, thinking seriously about running. My appearance at the GOP convention would be my chance to meet with activists and potential donors. I would be giving several speeches, including a prime speaking spot at a breakfast on Saturday morning. It would actually be better for me to have the distraction of the convention. Also, I argued, my appearances there had already been publicized. If I failed to show up, speculation about why I wasn't there would be unavoidable. We would lose that element of control over telling people about the diagnosis.

In the end, Frank relented, and we went to Sacramento. It was just one of countless acts of love and support he has shown me. My speaking engagements began virtually as soon as we arrived. The rest of the weekend was a whirlwind of introductions, receptions, and speeches. I was thankful to have something to concentrate on other than my health, although it was always in the back of my mind. The weekend was much more difficult for Frank. While I was busy, he spent his time on the phone telling our families the news. What frustrated him the most was how little he had to tell them. I was sick. Cancerous lymph nodes are not a good sign. And that is all we knew.

■ ■ ■

I had planned on the convention being something of a political coming-out party. I had anticipated saying "Yes!" when people asked me if I was going to run for the Senate. Now my cancer diagnosis forced me to be tentative. I no longer knew whether I was going to run. I didn't know whether I was going to be well enough or even alive. That weekend, instead of expressing energy and confidence in unseating Barbara Boxer, I thanked people for their interest and said I had yet to make up my mind.

Nevertheless, as California Republicans gathered in 2009, my changed circumstances didn't change the deep sense of unease I felt about my state. Pundits had begun to openly question whether California was a "failed state." We had the lowest bond rating of any state. Our per capita budget deficit was the highest in the nation. Not surprisingly, in the previous two decades almost four million more people had left California than had moved there from other states. High housing costs, bad schools, crumbling roads, and bleak job prospects were driving young, middle-class families to the exits. And high taxes and onerous regulatory burdens were forcing businesses to locate in other states.

The result was a "hollowing out" of the California middle class. The very rich and the very poor were staying, but the middle class was being driven out. Years later, this phenomenon and the inequality it creates would become issue number one for liberal Democrats, including President Obama. But it was already well under way in Democratic-ruled California in 2009. In 2012, I would be struck by how hypocritical it was when President Obama and liberal Democrats talked about rising income inequality and the hollowing out of the middle class as if these were the result of conservative policies. In fact, I saw in the state of California that they were the result of years of liberal policies.

If you had told me five years before, when I was CEO of Hewlett-Packard, that I would be contemplating running for the Senate in 2009, I would have laughed. In fact, I did laugh when people suggested I run for political office earlier in my career. But my experiences running a Fortune 20 company had taught me some things. I had learned valuable lessons about myself. I was comfortable with the choices I had made. I was, as well, secure in my accomplishments at HP. People had said some terrible things about me in a very public fashion. But when you go through something like that, you realize that what others say about you does not define you. Our choices and our actions—not others' words—define us. I had made mistakes, but I was comfortable that I had done what I thought was right, for the right reasons, to the very best of my ability. And so while the news of my dismissal raged on front pages all over the world, I was profoundly calm in the private knowledge that I had made it through the storm with my dignity and my conscience intact. As I wrote in the concluding pages of my memoir, *Tough Choices*, "My soul is my own and I am at peace."

I also knew how vulnerable businesses are to the long arm of the government. I had come into the job knowing that the employees were important and the customers were important. I knew I had a corporate board and shareholders to deal with. What I failed to understand was how much time and effort would go into dealing with government, either on the local, state, or federal level. Some in Congress, for example, came to the conclusion during my tenure that the Internet should be taxed. If we had taken our endless and endlessly complex tax code and applied it to the Internet, massive costs would be introduced into the system. And I knew that if this was an expensive prospect for HP, where I had hundreds of lawyers and accountants at my disposal to help navigate the government maze, it was a death sentence for thousands of small businesses.

That weekend in Sacramento I stood before the assembled California Republicans and gave them my perspective on their political world from my experience in the business world. Two things, above all, matter to me, I said: accountability and opportunity. From where I stood, no other issue separated the world of business and the world of government more than accountability. Years of fiscal mismanagement and political capture by the public employee unions in Sacramento had bankrupted the state of California. Washington was racking up unprecedented deficits. Congress has just passed the stimulus—a 1,000-page, $830 billion spending bill that no one actually read—so no one knew exactly where the money was going.

Imagine a business, I told the delegates, that asks for and receives more money each year, year after year. Now imagine that this same business has no metrics for performance or penalties for nonperformance. This business has no competitors, and the customers of this business have no choices. And finally, imagine a business that cannot tell investors where their money is going or how it is being spent. As taxpayers and citizens, I said, we are both investors in government and customers of it. Outside of government, no investor or customer would tolerate such a situation. They would demand accountability, transparency, and performance—and so should we.

As for opportunity, I knew firsthand how important that is. When those men gave me a chance to rise in that nine-person firm where I was a secretary, that was opportunity. But opportunity doesn't just happen. Government has the power to nurture or destroy it. California used to be a place that was open to an entrepreneur with a great idea to start a business. That's not the case anymore. California is ranked near dead last in the nation in states most hospitable to creating businesses. That's a self-inflicted wound. We have it in our power, I said, to make it easier for innovators, entrepreneurs, and small businessmen and -women to achieve their dreams and create jobs and opportunities—to unlock their potential for the benefit of us all. What we need is the leadership that unlocks that potential.

I had meant for that weekend to be the first step in a journey that would offer my political leadership to California. But life has a way of intruding on even the best-laid plans. As I made my case to the delegates about the state and the nation we were capable of being with the right leadership, I surveyed the crowd. Frank was nowhere to be found.

He was in the park outside, pacing back and forth and wondering why in the world I was giving a speech in Sacramento when I had just learned I had a disease with the power to take my life.

■ ■ ■

Driving home from Sacramento was therapeutic. The initial shock of the diagnosis had worn off, and the events of the weekend were behind us. The drive allowed Frank, Deborah, and me to formulate a plan for how to move forward. My greatest fear—and the fear that consumed Frank more than any other—was that the cancer had metastasized within my body. Not knowing what kind of cancer it was meant not knowing where it had begun. I darkly imagined my body riddled with tumors. We agreed that our first action item was to see my good friend and oncologist at Stanford Cancer Institute, Ranjana Advani. Ranjana's husband had worked with me at HP, and we had become friends. In the first of many, many kindnesses Ranjana showed me during my battle with cancer, she came to see me that Sunday after we returned from Sacramento. She examined me and told me that she didn't think my body was riddled with cancer. "I think this is breast cancer, and we can deal with it," she said. "The tests will prove me right or wrong, but that's what I think." I went to bed that night with a degree of reassurance.

At 6:30 Monday morning Frank and I were at Stanford Hospital to begin tests. The lump had been found in the lymph node under my arm, which meant that it could be many different kinds of cancer that had spread. So the doctors had to test for everything. The first test they performed was a full-body PET scan. I drank what felt like gallons of liquid and lay shivering in the cold for what felt like an eternity.

Many long days and multiple scans, MRIs, and mammograms later, we finally had a more definitive diagnosis: it was breast cancer, stage II. It hadn't been detected in the mammogram I had had weeks earlier, because the tumor in my left breast was very small. At the same time, the cancer was very aggressive and had spread to lymph nodes that are not captured in a mammogram. It was, without a doubt, a very close call. Later, after Obamacare was passed, the Health and Human Services Administration (HHS) changed the protocol for breast cancer screening. They recommended that women get a mammogram every other year and that they not do self-examinations. The Obama administration had concluded that this change in protocol would minimize false alarms and cost. I remember being insulted when HHS justified these changes by saying the old protocol created too much trauma and concern. Women are tough. We can handle it. I remember thinking that had I followed this protocol, I would probably be dead.

I had a tumor in the left breast and precancerous cells in my right breast. And although the cancer had spread to seven lymph nodes, my prognosis was excellent. The doctors recommended that I have a lumpectomy in both breasts to excise the cancerous tissue. Neither they nor I thought a mastectomy was necessary at the time—a decision I would later come to regret. They performed the surgery on March 2. I had decided previously to make the announcement that I had cancer at the time of my surgery. Given the speculation that I would run for Senate, I wanted to be sure to know exactly what we were dealing with before the news went public. Deborah put together a statement that we released that day.

Days later, I received crushing news from my doctors. The tissue removed during the surgery showed cancerous cells closer to the margins of the incisions than my doctors were comfortable with. Unless the margins were "clean," they couldn't be confident the cancer wouldn't return. The news meant that I would have to have more surgery, which would put off chemotherapy treatments.

The day of the second surgery was a low point. I remember lying on the gurney, alone, waiting to go into the operating room. Tears were streaming down my face. A nurse I didn't know came up to me, took my hand, and looked intently into my eyes. "I know you're having a really hard time," she said. "You're going to be okay." It was a simple gesture, but it had a great impact on me. It was the first of many kindnesses shown to me by strangers during my cancer journey. It was a moment of grace in the midst of a nightmare.

One of the most horrifying things about having cancer is that the doctors spend a lot of time telling you about all the risks and the downsides of the treatments they recommend. Patients who are already terrified about their disease are forced to sit and listen to everything that can go wrong from the treatment. As an example, my doctors recommended radiation treatment in addition to chemotherapy. They told me that while they thought I would tolerate radiation well, one of the risks of radiation is that it can cause secondary cancers. If I were to get a secondary cancer, they said, the situation would become very challenging.

Frank and I ended up feeling very burdened by all this information. My prognosis was excellent, but all the information I was getting focused on the bad. What saved me were two things. First, Ranjana was my guardian angel. Not only was she an oncologist, she was also a breast cancer survivor. She was able to help me keep my focus on the end game even if getting there was confusing and scary. Most of all, she was and is a wonderful, devoted friend. She accompanied me to every chemotherapy treatment. She stayed with me through difficult nights in the hospital—all while maintaining a busy medical practice. I owe her more than I can ever repay.

The second thing that got me through that difficult time was my old habit of gleaning as much information as I could and making an analytical judgment. I came to realize that the doctors were focusing on the possible downsides of treatment because they felt legally, ethically, and probably morally bound to do so. What the doctors were asking me to do was to assess the odds, to be a full participant in my treatment. And although it was burdensome at times, I am grateful for it. I was blessed to have highly competent, highly compassionate doctors: Dr. Robert Carlson, my oncologist, Dr. Fred Dirbas, my oncological surgeon, and Dr. Lauren Greenberg, my breast reconstruction surgeon. They knew me, they knew my case, and they felt free to propose whatever treatment they thought was best. Since then, I have worried that the passage of Obamacare threatens to sever this personal relationship between a patient and her doctor. When you are dealing with difficult news—like a life-threatening diagnosis—that relationship is everything. Your doctor is the person you trust, the person who has credibility, and the person who knows you. When bureaucratic rules and cost considerations come in between you and your doctor, your care suffers. Peace of mind—or worse—is lost.

■ ■ ■

Going in, the thing I was most afraid of about cancer was chemotherapy. I knew how grueling it could be—or at least I thought I did. I worried about my ability to stand up to the fatigue, the nausea, and the other nasty side effects. My doctors had told me that my excellent physical condition would allow me to tolerate treatment well, and they prescribed an aggressive schedule—eight rounds of chemotherapy over four months. We had put it off once for the second surgery. Now, to my great dismay, my doctors told me they were still not confident that the lumpectomy had removed enough tissue. I would need another surgery, they said, but chemotherapy could no longer wait. I had to begin treatment with the knowledge that when it was over, I would undergo surgery number three.

Chemotherapy did not disappoint me. In the course of four months, I was hospitalized three times. The first visit was to receive massive infusions of fluids. Like many chemo patients, I had become dangerously dehydrated as the result of being unable to keep anything down. The second hospitalization was when I developed pneumonia. The third stay, also not uncommon among people undergoing chemotherapy, was for blood transfusions. My heart was also weakened during the treatment and stopped pumping properly. We had to stop the treatment while I went on heart medications. It was a very, very difficult period. I had always been a very healthy and active person. During chemotherapy, I wondered whether I would ever feel like myself again. When my health finally returned, it was a most delicious feeling. I savor that feeling of health and well-being to this day. Whenever I don't want to hit the gym, I take a deep breath and remember the days when I couldn't walk more than a single block. That's all the motivation I need. My health is a blessing and a gift that I hope I will never again take for granted.

When in late July my third surgery failed to satisfy my doctors with its results, I had had enough. Together with my excellent doctors, Frank and I had given it our best shot, but it was over. I did then what I wish I had been psychologically prepared to do at the beginning: I decided to have a bilateral mastectomy. I don't question the wisdom of doctors who seek to spare women's breasts and recommend lumpectomies—nor do I for a second fault women who select that option. I simply couldn't continue the path that I was on. I underwent the surgery in August.

That September I was scheduled to be on a panel of cancer survivors at Fortune's Most Powerful Women Summit in San Diego. Because I was still undergoing daily radiation treatments, I was forced to appear by remote video. Elizabeth Edwards, whose breast cancer had returned and metastasized, also appeared by video. I told the gathering that I was one of the lucky ones, and I meant it. Not only was I beating the cancer, the fight through surgery, chemotherapy, and radiation had made me acutely aware of my blessings. I was blessed to live near one of the best cancer centers in the country at Stanford University. And I was blessed to have had the opportunity to face my fears, work through them, and move forward with renewed confidence and enthusiasm.

Above all else, I am blessed to be completely cancer free. I have now passed my five-year mark, a key milestone for anyone who has been touched by cancer. My wonderful doctors at the George Washington University Medical Faculty Associates, Dr. Rachel Brem, Dr. Christine Teal, Dr. Nancy Gaba, and Dr. Gigi El-Bayoumi, have pronounced my health "perfect."

When I ran for the U.S. Senate I would often joke that after chemotherapy, Barbara Boxer and politics didn't seem so scary. As my radiation treatments came to an end, I was now more certain than ever that I would follow my adventure as the first female CEO of a Fortune 20 company with a new adventure: throwing my hat into the political ring and taking on the liberal champion of the most liberal state in the union. It was a battle worth fighting, and I was unafraid.

Other than my mother dying, I thought being fired as the chief executive officer of Hewlett-Packard on the front pages of the world's newspapers was the worst thing that could ever happen to me. Little did I know that life would have greater challenges in store for me. Still, although I would not wish cancer on anyone, I am genuinely grateful for the path I have traveled. I had come to know, in profound ways, the power of love, the comfort of friendship, the redemption of faith, and the kindness of strangers.

CHAPTER 4

Annus Horribilis

A S ANY SURVIVOR KNOWS, GOING THROUGH an experience like fighting cancer is transformative, although not altogether negative. Your immediate worry is for yourself and the people you love. Later, when the disease is in retreat, comes a feeling, not of triumph, but of calm, discerning perspective. Your time horizon goes from very short to very long. You're pulled from worrying about whether you'll be alive in the next six months to worrying about what kind of country your grandchildren will inherit. Suddenly, for me, running for the Senate was no longer just a cold calculation of the odds of beating Barbara Boxer. It was a rare chance to change the order of things for the better.

As the summer began and I was convinced that I could survive chemotherapy, I slowly turned my attention back to the race. When I was well enough to actually sit up and talk on the phone, I called potential supporters from my home in Silicon Valley. Their responses were consistently encouraging but came with a serious caveat: it would be a hard, uphill battle. Unbowed and more than a little clueless, Deborah Bowker and I moved forward. In between visits to Stanford Hospital to have a cocktail of poison pumped into my veins, we began to put together a campaign team.

It was certainly not the first time—nor would it be the last—that Deborah proved herself indispensable. Both of us naively believed that the better candidate—with the better team and the better message—would win. So we set out to build a campaign befitting a citizen legislator: one that didn't play politics as usual but talked directly to the people; one that was faithful to its mission, but didn't take itself too seriously. A campaign, we both agreed, that would be both consequential and *fun*.

I was too sick to be out and about, so Deborah was my eyes and my ears. She and I would sit on rocking chairs in back of my house and talk for hours about what kind of campaign we wanted to run. Slowly the team took shape. We wanted to hire as many Californians as we could. Longtime California businessman Gary Hunt agreed to be our campaign finance chairman. We stole a bright young lawyer from Senator Kay Bailey Hutchison,

Arjun Mody, to be our policy director. Julie Soderland came from Arnold Schwarzenegger's press team to head up our communications. And because California is a state where paid media is critical, we took our time choosing a media consultant. I knew Fred Davis—another longtime Californian—from the McCain campaign. He was the creativity behind the famous "Celebrity" ad that compared Barack Obama with Paris Hilton and Britney Spears during the 2008 campaign. Deborah spent hours with Fred and came away convinced that he would bring a fresh perspective to my candidacy. So we hired him. And he did.

Our campaign manager, it turned out, didn't wait to be recruited—he came to us. Longtime Sacramento strategist Marty Wilson approached us after watching Senator Boxer preemptively attack me and my record at Hewlett-Packard throughout the summer of 2009. I wasn't yet a candidate, but the Boxer team was taking no chances. They circulated a hit piece on my tenure at HP from a defunct business magazine. Marty was so mad he got in touch with Deborah, who was so mad she hired him to begin the counterattack before I had the chance to meet him.

And as she often does, Barbara Boxer helped us make the case against her. While I was still deep in chemo land in June, a video went viral that reminded California voters why Barbara Boxer had been in Washington, D.C., too long. The video showed Boxer in a committee hearing questioning Brigadier General Michael Walsh of the Army Corps of Engineers. As the general attempts to answer one of Boxer's questions, she interrupts him in mid-sentence to insist that he call her "senator" instead of the respectful "ma'am" he had been using.

"It's just a thing," she said. "I worked so hard to get that title, so I'd appreciate it." The video showed Barbara Boxer at her prickly, out-of-touch, imperious worst. And when the Rasmussen poll came out in August, it showed me, the noncandidate, running neck and neck with Boxer. Forty-five percent of those polled supported Boxer's reelection and 41 percent supported me. The senator's "very favorable" rating had sunk even lower, to 21 percent.* Buoyed, we took our first official step toward being a candidate and registered a campaign committee—Carly for California—on August 18.

■ ■ ■

The filing of our campaign committee set off a fresh round of speculation in the media about how the crop of California GOP candidates might be changing in 2010. Officially, I was still just mulling the run. More certain of her plans was former eBay CEO Meg Whitman. On September 22, Meg formally announced her campaign for the GOP nod to challenge California Democratic gover-

---

*Dan Walters, "As Campaign Looms, Boxer Shaky Again," *Sacramento Bee*, August 10, 2009.

nor Jerry Brown. Meg's announcement was no surprise. I had known of her plans to run for governor since the McCain campaign. She had reportedly already spent $15 million on her campaign and had said she was prepared to spend as much as $150 million of her own money on the race.

The press immediately picked up on the narrative of two women, both former Silicon Valley CEOs, both political neophytes, potentially running for higher office in California. From then on, the public and even much of the media constantly confused our two candidacies. Part of the problem was the preconceptions people had about Silicon Valley CEOs. They assumed I wasn't conservative because I lived in the Bay Area and worked in the Valley. The truth is, the confusion was problematic for both of us. Despite our surface similarities, there were real differences between Meg and me. I am pro-life, for example, whereas Meg is pro-choice. Sometimes the confusion wasn't quite so serious. Meg and I are married to two very accomplished but very different men. I remember a voter approaching me at an event and asking, "So your husband is a neurosurgeon?" To which I replied, no, that's Meg's husband. Mine actually started out as a tow truck driver.

Even as we were taking our first steps toward becoming a candidate, I was still dealing with the effects of my cancer. For much of the fall I was undergoing daily radiation treatments, which limited my travel to locales that allowed me to be at Stanford Hospital every morning. Still, I managed to get out on day trips to visit California communities. Outwardly I was doing all the things I needed to do to prepare to run. I was traveling when I could, meeting donors, and filling out my campaign team.

It was in the midst of this, on October 12, 2009, that we learned of Lori's death. For the second time in nine months, time stopped. We had spent the last months of her life desperately trying to intervene with her doctors to make sure they understood the depths of her illness. Because of the way privacy laws are written, we couldn't learn anything from Lori's doctors that she didn't want us to know. Finally, we found a doctor who kindly told us she could listen, although she could not tell us anything. But by then it was too late.

I have thought often since then of how poorly we deal with mental illness and addiction as a nation. Like Lori, those who are ill frequently fight against help. Medical privacy laws, although perhaps well intentioned, make it easier for an addict to continue down a destructive path. These laws make it very difficult for those who worry that a loved one is a danger to themselves or others to get the help so desperately needed. They also make it difficult for concerned physicians to raise a warning flag. And criminalizing addictions, or minimizing the devastating impact of mental illness on families and communities, only makes these problems worse.

We had pleaded with Lori to move closer to her family

in those last months. But as many addicts do, she literally ran away from the people trying to help her. She insisted on moving to New Jersey. In my last conversation with her on the phone, I begged her again to let us get her help. She put me off. Now all I could think of, staring at the policemen standing in my living room, was what else I could have done to save her.

In the throes of shock and sorrow that felt as deep as an ocean, as well as a dull anger over what had become of Lori, I planned a funeral. I chose her favorite flower— stargazer lilies like the ones she had carried in her bridal bouquet.

I labored especially over her Mass card. What should all those who came to express their condolences and support leave with in their hands to remember her by? In the end, we chose the Serenity Prayer for one side:

> God grant me the serenity to accept the things I cannot change, the courage to change the things I can, and the wisdom to know the difference.

On the other, a verse that gave us all some peace and seemed so much like the daughter we deeply loved:

I'm Free

Don't grieve for me, for now I'm free.
I'm following the path God laid for me.
I took His hand when I heard His call.

I turned my back and left it all.

I could not stay another day, to laugh, to love, to
work or play.

Tasks left undone must stay that way, I found that
peace at close of day.

If my parting has left a void, then fill it with
remembered joy.

A friendship shared, a laugh, a kiss, ah yes, these
things I too will miss.

Be not burdened with times of sorrow, I wish you
the sunshine of tomorrow.

My life's been full, I've savored much—good
friends, good times, a loved one's touch.

Perhaps my time was all too brief, don't lengthen it
now with undue grief.

Lift up your hearts and share with me—God
wanted me now, He set me free.*

We buried her on a Friday in Pittsburgh. Frank
wanted her in the family plot where his mother and father were buried. Tracy, her husband, Lowell, Frank, and
I drove up from Virginia, leaving the grandkids with
Lowell's parents. And as we went through the rituals of
saying good-bye to Lori, people said the usual, kind
things. At her funeral, friends and family told me she
was in a better place. I truly believed it, and that faith allowed me to survive.

Although I had always believed in God, as I grew

---

*Frank and I first encountered "I'm Free" in the days after Lori died and it
spoke to me. We were unable to identify the author but remain in his or her
debt.

older my faith became more abstract. I still prayed every day, but I had come to view God as something of a super CEO of a massive enterprise. He had created the universe and put in place a sophisticated set of management processes that kept things running, not necessarily smoothly, but the way He intended them over the long arc of time. He didn't attend to every detail. He didn't know every person—how could He possibly? The virgin birth, the resurrection, the divinity of Jesus Christ, the Holy Spirit—all were powerful allegories to draw people toward the right path. These were profound ideas at the heart of a sophisticated governance system, but they weren't actually real. Or so I thought.

Later, with the help of Bill Hybels, the pastor of Willow Creek Community Church in South Barrington, Illinois, I came to a deeper connection with God and my faith in Him. I came to see the signs that were all around me of God's personal presence in our lives. Many of them came from the worlds of science and technology, where I had made my professional career. Scientists had discovered the miracle of millions of new life forms in the depths of the ocean, some in places so dark and inhospitable that no one had imagined life could survive, much less thrive. Why not, then, the miracle of a virgin birth? Were there not inexplicable mysteries that confronted us every day? Were physicists not still struggling to understand the basic building blocks of the universe? Were quarks and protons and dark matter not profoundly miraculous? Did Einstein not prove that energy never dies, it merely changes form?

And of course God knew every single one of us personally and kept track of us and heard our prayers. Every time I turned on the GPS in my car, I would marvel at the human ingenuity that built a system that keeps precise track of where we are, knows when we deviate off course, and provides clear instructions as to how to return to the right path. We may ignore those instructions—we may even become annoyed at the voice telling us to turn right in a thousand feet. Nevertheless, guidance is provided. If human beings can do this, then certainly God knows everything that is happening in the universe—not in broad management strokes, but in minute, personal detail.

When my mother died a decade earlier, I didn't have this personal connection with God, and her death shattered me. When Lori died, my personal relationship with Jesus Christ saved me. While struggling to make funeral arrangements under the weight of my own feelings, I watched Frank closely. We were both suffocating with grief and guilt, but his suffering, I knew, was worse than mine. Later, when Frank told me he had lost his faith, I was not surprised. It would be months before he once again felt the comfort of God's presence, but he would find it again. Having that knowledge would have eased the awful pain of that time. All I knew then was that the faith that sustained me had left Frank. Somehow we made it through the weekend.

■ ■ ■

Frank and I talked for days about what to do next. We talked about ending the campaign for the Senate. Ultimately both of us decided that the choices being made in Washington and their impact on other people's lives were important and worth our effort. And so we continued.

We chose November 4—one day shy of a year before the general election—to make our announcement. To highlight the problems facing California's family-owned businesses, we joined the owner and employees of Earth Friendly Products in their warehouse in Garden Grove, California, just south of Los Angeles. Earth Friendly Products is a manufacturer of environmentally friendly cleaning products started by a Greek immigrant, Van Vlahakis. We were running a campaign to put the American Dream within reach of more Californians, and Vlahakis had lived the American Dream. He came to the United States from Greece when he was eighteen, with twenty-two dollars in his pocket. He built a business that produces more than 150 products at five manufacturing plants—all in the United States. The largest is in California.

I began the announcement the way I would begin public appearances for weeks to come—by addressing the issue of my hair. It had fallen out from the chemotherapy, of course. I wore a wig for a time to cover up the scrubby, gray fuzz that was slowly returning, but eventually I ditched it in favor of the natural look. I had come through a great trial, and now I was staring another challenge in the face. Hair didn't seem that important.

After assuring the audience that my cancer was behind me, I got to the point. Californians were reeling under the effects of decades of failed leadership. High taxes, overregulation, and big bureaucracies were killing jobs in California. After three terms in the Senate, Barbara Boxer had showed no inclination to reverse course. "I believe the people of California are ready to say hello to a political newcomer who actually knows how to get something done," I said.

I had also written an op-ed in the *Orange County Register* to introduce myself to voters and to address a painful topic. Two months earlier, it had been revealed that I had a spotty record of voting in elections in the previous decades. I had always registered as a Republican, but I had not always voted. I was embarrassed, and I had no good excuse. I told the voters as much. "For many years I felt disconnected from the decisions made in Washington, and, to be honest, really didn't think my vote mattered because I didn't have a direct line of sight from my vote to a result," I wrote. I was wrong. My experience in business and serving on advisory boards in government had taught me how profoundly the decisions being made in Washington affect every family and every business. That was the reason I was running for the Senate. The long arm of government was inescapable as never before and the people were hurting as never before. Californians deserved better.

As Thanksgiving approached, what had been a terrible year was coming to a blessed end. Frank's sixtieth birthday was coming in December, but we had decided to celebrate it early, on the Saturday of the holiday weekend, so the family could be together. Months before, I had decided to throw him a big party—a kind of "this is your life" event featuring friends from throughout his sixty years. Of course, I was sick from surgery and chemo at the time, but I came up with what I thought was a pretty clever way to still plan the party. I would lie in bed and ask Frank to come talk to me to pass the time. Because I was sick, he would be patient and sit by my bedside. I steered the conversation toward stories about his childhood and his years at AT&T. Then, when he left, I took out a notebook I had hidden under the covers and wrote down the names and events he had mentioned.

Working this way, I colluded with his sisters in Pittsburgh to identify and locate friends from throughout Frank's life, from the old neighborhood he grew up in and drove a tow truck through, to the offices of AT&T, where he rose from technician to executive. We booked the main dining room of an old train station in Pittsburgh that had been converted into a restaurant. We had a Temptations-style singing group. We had a Marilyn Monroe impersonator. We had six different birthday cakes. We even found the car Frank used to talk about all the time when I first met him—his first car, a 396 Super

Sport Chevelle. Frank's nephew, who owned the body shop started by Frank's father, fixed it up like new. It was my gift to him.

When Thanksgiving came, we went to Washington to be with Tracy and her family. That Saturday, we all drove up to Pittsburgh. Frank thought his family was getting together for a low-key celebration of his big day. When he walked into a restaurant, there were 150 people there waiting for him, some he hadn't seen for forty years. Frank was overwhelmed. That night I was reminded of many things throughout our life. Chief among them was how very fortunate Frank and I were despite the pain we had suffered. We had been able to throw a big birthday bash at a time when we desperately needed something happy in our lives. Not everyone is so lucky.

It had been six weeks since Lori died. I had seriously contemplated canceling the party. My beloved sisters-in-law, Claudia and Ursula, counseled against this. In the end, I agreed. We needed to celebrate life, which is for the living and about moving forward. As I watched Frank's face that night, I knew I had made the right decision. He felt loved and affirmed and celebrated. And all his family and friends knew that he had been, and remains to this day, the blessing and the rock of my life.

For the first time, I allowed myself to think there might be blue sky ahead.

CHAPTER 5

Meet Me in Mendota

I HAD NEVER SEEN DEBORAH SO ANGRY. IT WAS January 14, 2010. That day the weekslong speculation that former GOP congressman Tom Campbell would quit the California governor's race and enter the Senate race ceased to be rumor and became fact. Suddenly, the race for the chance to unseat Barbara Boxer was transformed.

When I announced my candidacy two months earlier, I had joined a field of one. Chuck Devore was a thoughtful, earnest state assemblyman from Irvine and a selfproclaimed Tea Party Republican. He'd been in the race for a year at that point, traveling throughout the state, mostly by car, carefully logging his visits as he went. He had, by his count, over one hundred campaign stops under his belt by the time I announced my candidacy, but he had been able to raise only seven hundred thousand dollars in a race the pundits were saying would cost thirty million dollars or more. I knew better than to take anything for granted, but I was confident I had the conservative principles and the team to prevail in a head-to-head contest with Chuck Devore.

There was no doubt that Tom Campbell complicated this calculus. He had already run unsuccessfully for the U.S. Senate twice, losing in the Republican primary for the chance to take on Boxer in 1992 and then later, decisively, in a general election contest against Democratic senator Dianne Feinstein in 2000. Reportedly, Campbell had come to the conclusion he couldn't compete in a GOP gubernatorial primary in which Meg Whitman and state insurance commissioner Steve Poizner were self-financing to the tune of tens of millions of dollars. So Campbell switched—or was pushed—to the Senate race.

Tom Campbell was a likeable, amiable fellow. As a perennial candidate and a former congressman, he came to the Senate race with relatively high voter identification. Unlike Chuck Devore and me, the voters knew his name. As a result, he was the instant front-runner in a competitive race. When the Field Poll came out in late January, it showed Campbell leading me by 5 points and Chuck Devore by 24 points. Thirty-nine percent of likely Republican voters were undecided.*

The fact that few California voters knew who I was made it imperative that I define myself to them before my competition had the chance to do so. It was a year in which President Obama's record deficits and a big government health care bill were on the ballot alongside Democratic candidates. The Tea Party had risen up to challenge the direction the country was moving in. Republican voters were feeling then, much as they are today, that they had been duped. They had compromised their principles in order to win elections and been burned in the process. Then came Scott Brown's startling success in the race to succeed Ted Kennedy. His victory in deep blue Massachusetts underscored the national dissatisfaction with liberal governance in Washington, D.C., not just among conservatives but independents as well.

Tom Campbell's theory of the race was that he was that elusive political figure: the socially moderate, fiscally conservative Republican. He was both pro-choice and pro–gay marriage but ostensibly conservative when it came to taxing and spending. This mix, it was argued, would make him more palatable to California voters than your average Republican. The problem with this theory was that Campbell's record didn't back it up. In 2009, when he

*Carla Marinucci, "Campbell Leads New Field Poll on GOP Senate Race," *San Francisco Chronicle*, January 21, 2010.

was still a gubernatorial candidate, he had proposed a supposedly "temporary" thirty-two-cents-a-gallon gasoline tax. He also supported a ballot proposition—defeated overwhelmingly by California voters—that would have extended another ostensibly temporary hike in sales taxes, income taxes, and vehicle licensing fees. All these taxes, he explained, were necessary to compensate for state budget deficits. I had a distinctly different view. I didn't believe the way to close budget deficits was to raise taxes but to control spending.

Still, I agreed with Tom Campbell in one sense: I believed that fiscal issues—and the jobs they either promote or destroy—were on the minds of voters in 2010. Campbell's candidacy played into the conventional wisdom that said conservatives who also care about social issues couldn't compete in California. On the stump, I didn't hide my traditional values on life and marriage. I was always careful to explain that I understood and respected that not everyone agreed with me, but I was a proud socially *and* fiscally conservative candidate—so much so, in fact, that pundits confidently predicted that I would have to move to the left if I won the primary and faced Barbara Boxer.

I held these principles as a matter of conviction, not politics. I could no more shed my views than I could shed my background as a businesswoman. And this, I believed, was the strength I brought to public service. I had come from a world in which accountability and results trumped spin and message control. It's not possible to reinvent yourself or fudge your positions when hundreds of thousands of employees and shareholders are scrutinizing your every move. I had come from a world with a bottom line, and that separated me from both my competitors.

My campaign had two objectives in the primary: first, to introduce me to the voters as a solutions-oriented non-politician who knows how to create the conditions in which people and jobs thrive. Second, we planned to keep our message focused on Barbara Boxer's failed tenure in Washington. It was this latter part of our plan that Tom Campbell's entry into the race complicated. The media narrative quickly congealed into a three-way contest in which Devore was the conservative candidate, Campbell was the politically acceptable one, and I was the rich dilettante. It became clear to me that we needed to push back—to show the media, the voters, and our opponents that we meant business.

My campaign manager, Marty Wilson, huddled with our media consultant, Fred Davis, and came to me with an idea. What if we made a memorable but low-cost ad that would be distributed on the Internet but not on television? The idea was to make an ad that created enough buzz to attract viewers on the Internet and also generate press coverage on television—all at no additional cost to the campaign. I liked the idea, both because it leveraged our resources and because it was daring and unconventional. So I agreed. The result was the so-called demon sheep video, the most talked about ad of the political cycle.

The message of the three-and-a-half minute video was that Tom Campbell was not who he was portraying himself to be. It opened with sheep grazing peacefully in a meadow. Suddenly, the skies darken and the music turns ominous. As the narrator describes Campbell's history of support for higher taxes and higher spending, a man appears on screen on all fours wearing an ill-fitting sheep costume, with red, glowing eyes. The tagline: "Is Tom Campbell the fiscal conservative he claims to be, or is he a FCINO—a fiscal conservative in name only?"

Whether you loved it or hated it—and there were plenty of people on both sides, even within my campaign—the ad more than accomplished its objective. In a state where it cost about one million dollars to run an ad on television for a week, our fifteen-thousand-dollar video was broadcast nationwide on cable television and was viewed more than half a million times on YouTube. The hashtag #demonsheep trended on Twitter. It spawned more than one Web site and more bad puns in headlines than we could count. There was a lot of shaking of heads and criticism of the ad, but my feeling was we were an untraditional campaign announcing ourselves in an untraditional way. Rather than back away from the ad, we promised more informative and entertaining media to come.

In the weeks that followed, campaigning began to settle into a routine. What people didn't know was that for most of that period, while we were keeping a relentless campaign schedule, I was dealing with a severely pain-ful consequence of my cancer from the year before.

In the course of my bilateral mastectomy that past August—at almost precisely the same time we registered our campaign with the FEC—the surgeon had implanted expanders in my chest in anticipation of reconstruction surgery. In September I underwent radiation therapy. What I would come to understand later was that the ra-diation treatments toughened the skin the expanders were meant to stretch. In December 2009 my doctors began the process of inflating the expanders. Every few weeks I would go in and have air injected into them (it-self not a walk in the park!). Following each expansion, I would experience excruciating pain. This went on throughout the first part of 2010. I remember being in so much pain before a debate at the Reagan Library that I took a pain pill beforehand, even though pain pills make me nauseated. I threw up before the debate, and I threw up after it. In between, I sat on a stool under the televi-sion lights and prayed to God I wouldn't do it again. It was only later I realized that every time I went in to have the expanders inflated, my ribs were cracking as my skin refused to stretch sufficiently.

On the campaign trail, my number one priority was getting Californians back to work. At each stop, I made a practice of appearing at a family-owned business and having the business owner introduce me. Senator Boxer was in Washington talking up the supposedly job-

creating effects of the president's budget-busting stimulus bill. The president's advisers had claimed that the bill
would keep unemployment from rising higher than 8
percent. I spent my days visiting the fifteen metro areas
where the unemployment rate was over 15 percent and
the eight counties with jobless rates that topped 20 percent. My message was that borrowed money and massive
bureaucracy cannot create jobs. Only innovation, energy,
and the optimism of entrepreneurs can do that.

I visited a cement plant in Colton, California, in San
Bernardino County, about sixty miles east of Los Angeles.
The plant was one of the largest employers in the area. It
had been in operation since 1891 but had stopped manufacturing cement in November 2009 because the price of
cement couldn't keep pace with the costs of new environmental regulations forced on the plant by the state of California. Almost one hundred workers had lost their jobs.

It was, I said, painful proof of the failure of the belief
held by Senator Boxer and her liberal allies that government spending alone could create jobs and prosperity.
The stimulus had promised lots of "shovel ready" jobs,
but what did California have to show for the $862 billion
price tag? "You can't build much without cement," I said.
"And yet here this plant sits virtually idle."

We worked slowly and steadily to introduce me to the
California electorate, and we kept our focus on the general election. For the next couple months, the public polls
showed that Boxer was vulnerable. When matched up

against either Campbell or me, it was essentially a tie. And although the primary polling continued to show Campbell in the lead, a large percentage of the electorate remained undecided. Voters were not yet tuning in to the race. When they did we were determined to be ready.

At the Republican Party Convention in mid-March, we delivered on our promise to provide more interesting and educational media than your run-of-the-mill political campaign. We unveiled another Fred Davis creation, this time a nearly eight-minute video with a tongue-in-cheek depiction of Barbara Boxer as a hot air blimp, ceaselessly talking and floating over Washington. The visuals were light, but the message was deadly serious: Barbara Boxer had been in Washington too long. She was out of touch with California. Once again, Fred had perfectly captured the feelings of the voters. "It's not Washington that's broken," I told the convention. "It is the detached and arrogant leadership in Washington that is broken. It is the destructive elitism that captures Washington that is broken."

We continued hammering on the theme of an inside-Washington, cronyist elite that was indifferent to the plight of California workers and families. As more voters heard my message, the polls began to tighten. By the end of March, Campbell and I were tied within the margin of error. In April we went up with our first television ad of the campaign. The spot detailed my rise from secretary to CEO and ended with me speaking straight into the camera: "Let's stop sending Washington more of our money, and let's make sure they spend our money wisely and well. I have faith that working together we can actually get something done."

Our campaign continued to gain momentum as the June 8 primary neared. In early May I received the endorsement of Sarah Palin in a post on her Facebook page. I was gratified for her support at that crucial time. I also received the endorsement of the National Right to Life Committee and the Susan B. Anthony List, a national group that supports pro-life female candidates. I was honored to have their support.

We spent those last, critical weeks of the campaign making the case to the voters that I was the candidate with the experience and the integrity to unseat Barbara Boxer. The Campbell campaign did the same thing; however, as had happened in his previous campaigns, he was forced to suspend his television advertising at critical points because of lack of funds.

As candidates began to vote by mail three weeks before the primary, we began to see our efforts bear fruit. A *Los Angeles Times*/USC poll in late May showed that we had gained important ground with women and both moderate and conservative voters. My share of women voters had risen from 21 percent in March to 40 percent. I had gained 15 percent of self-identified moderates and was now tied with Tom Campbell for his base. And the poll showed I had a full 43 percent of the conservative vote. When election day finally came, it wasn't even close. I won with

56 percent of the vote, besting Tom Campbell by 34 points and Chuck Devore by 37 points.

Election night wasn't so much of a victory as it was a pause. As I spoke to the crowd at our rally in Irvine, I congratulated my primary opponents for a race well run. And as I looked forward to the race yet to come, I found myself reflecting on the belief in human potential that had sustained me since I was a little girl. It is the same belief that motivates me in all that I do today. That night I told the crowd that this belief in human potential is what will be on the ballot in the fall.

"This election is about big differences between the kind of people we are and what we believe," I said. "I believe that each person everywhere has enormous potential if they are given the freedom and the opportunity to fulfill it. Barbara Boxer believes that it is government that promotes potential, not the individual."

Ken Khachigian, a former speechwriter for Ronald Reagan and one of the authors of Richard Nixon's memoirs, had written those words. I usually write my own speeches, but Ken had a way with words that I frequently found irresistible. He advised me throughout my campaign as a mentor and a friend. He is wise in the way of California politics. He knew a conservative victory in California was a long shot but worth fighting for. To this day, he calls me Jedi. I call him Yoda.

That night, just hours after I was declared the winner, Barbara Boxer challenged me to a series of debates. The next day at the Republican victory rally in Anaheim, I responded: "Barbara, I'll debate you anytime, anywhere. As far as I'm concerned, we can debate once a week." I had only one condition.

"Meet me in Mendota, Barbara," I said. "Come see the faces of the people whose lives have been destroyed."

■ ■ ■

No issue loomed larger for me in my campaign against Senator Boxer than water. Water means life, which in California means farming, which means jobs. What was happening in the summer of 2010 in California was a man-made drought in the Central Valley that was killing jobs. It was an ongoing human tragedy of our own making. We had it in our power to end the tragedy. The only question, I repeatedly put to the voters, was this: which do we think is more important, families or fish?

The water that traditionally gave life to the most productive farmland in the world in California's Central Valley came from the mountains north and east of Sacramento thanks to a network of dams, pumping stations, and canals. In 2006 a collection of environmental groups filed a lawsuit demanding that the federal government close the water spigot to the Central Valley to save a three-inch fish called the delta smelt. The environmentalists charged that the number of smelt in the waters of the Sacramento–San Joaquin River Delta was declining because too much mountain water was being diverted to the Central Valley farms. In 2007 a federal judge agreed. The next year the federal government issued a "biological opinion" under the Endangered Species Act decreeing that 150 billion gallons of water be diverted away from the farms and out into the Pacific Ocean. Another biological opinion in 2009, this one directed at populations of salmon and steelhead, slowed the water flow even more. On the basis of these two decrees, hundreds of thousands of acres of farmland were destroyed along with the lives of thousands of the farmers who worked them.

California has always had droughts. The difference now was that the actions of the government were making the droughts much worse. For forty years, even as the population doubled, the state failed to add a new storage or water conveyance system. Environmentalists prevented the building of new dams and aqueducts. The result is that an astonishing 70 percent of the rainfall in a given year rushes out of the California mountains and into the sea. The biological opinions issued by the federal government in 2007 and 2009 made the situation even worse.

By the fall of 2009, the farm economy of the Central Valley had been devastated. In the areas affected by the water restrictions, unemployment reached as high as 15 percent. At the center of this devastation was Mendota, once celebrated as the "Cantaloupe Center of the

World" and now derided as the "Detroit of California." The government-created drought and the foreclosure crisis had combined to produce a truly stratospheric unemployment rate. Almost 40 percent of Mendota residents were out of work. Crime, food lines, and alcohol and drug abuse became rampant in an area that once was famous for producing almonds, plums, corn, bell peppers, tomatoes, and melons.

I traveled to Mendota for the first time early in the primary. The hollow, hopeless eyes of the men I met there stayed with me. And the wasted human potential of their lives came to represent, for me, the wider economic challenges facing California. Here were men and families hurting through no fault of their own. Here was a community that lived at the mercy of lawyers, judges, and bureaucrats from thousands of miles away. Here, in Mendota, was a human tragedy that was entirely preventable. In Mendota, just as elsewhere in California, we weren't just going through tough economic times. We were actively destroying jobs through government policies. Like all human beings, the men and women of the Central Valley deserved the opportunity and the tools to fulfill their potential and live lives of dignity. What their so-called leaders were offering—when they bothered to pay attention—were lives of dependence on the whims of bureaucrats.

No one was better positioned to change the lives of the people of Mendota than Barbara Boxer. She was chairman of the Senate Environment and Public Works Committee in a Democratic-controlled Congress. Congress has the power to suspend portions of the Endangered Species Act when it deems it in the public interest. And yet Senator Boxer, with an eye toward her political patrons in the radical environmental community, refused to act. In the summer of 2009, South Carolina senator Jim DeMint introduced legislation that would have suspended implementation of the two biological opinions and turned the water spigots back on in the Central Valley. Senator Boxer—along with California's other Democratic senator, Dianne Feinstein—voted against the bill. Even when Senator Feinstein came around and proposed legislation in February 2010 to loosen restrictions on water to the farmland, Boxer refused to stand with her. To me, this made it crystal clear where Senator Boxer's priorities were. She said she was fighting for Californians, but it sure looked like she was fighting for another six years in Washington by continuing to bow to the demands of extreme environmentalists. I made the promise that if I were elected to the Senate, the first thing I would do is go see Senator Feinstein and say, "Let's turn the water back on."

The tragedy is that the crisis in the Central Valley continues to this day—and the ongoing drought in California has made the situation that much more dire. As recently as 2014, Dianne Feinstein, in the midst of another horrible drought, went to Barbara Boxer to enlist her in helping the people of the Central Valley. Once again, Senator Boxer refused. Predictably, some people blame global warming for the crisis, but when you drive along I-5 through the farm country, the hand-painted signs that dot the freeway make clear whom the farmers see as the culprit. There's this:

FARM WATER CUT

50% cut 2010
60% cut 2009
65% cut 2008

= HIGHER FOOD COST!

And this:

No water = No food
No water = No jobs
No water = No future*

Throughout the campaign, I repeated my request to Senator Boxer to meet me in Mendota—to see, up close and personal, the impact of the imposition of her ideology on the people of the Central Valley. She never did meet me there. What she and President Obama have offered instead is sadly typical of the worldview that governs too many in Washington today. They've chosen to

---

*Daniel Wood, "California Drought: Farmers Cut Back Sharply, Affecting Jobs and Food Supply," *Christian Science Monitor*, February 19, 2014.

manage a bad situation rather than provide the leadership to change it. They haven't given the people of the Central Valley the opportunity and the tools to build better futures. They've only offered them government aid to make their meager existence less miserable. President Obama announced help in 2014 in the form of a $1 billion "Climate Resilience Fund" to combat the effects of "climate change," including funding for food banks in the area. For the president to blame the situation in the Central Valley on global warming is the height of hypocrisy, arrogance, and willful disregard for other people. Liberals love to tell us how much they care. What they never mention is the crushed potential of those whose livelihoods their policies have destroyed.

■ ■ ■

While Tom Campbell, Chuck Devore, and I had been slugging it out in the primary, Barbara Boxer had been busy building a war chest to use against the eventual Republican victor. Thanks in part to two fund-raising visits to California by President Obama in the spring of 2010, Boxer had a whopping $10 million on hand as I emerged from the primary. When she filed her second-quarter fund-raising reports that July, she had raised $4.6 million in just the last three months, more than any other candidate, Republican or Democrat. That brought her total up to $11.3 million, twelve times the amount of cash my campaign had in the bank.* In sharp contrast to her bank account, the polls showed Boxer with less of an advantage in the minds of voters. A Rasmussen poll released just after the primary showed Senator Boxer with a 5-point lead, at 48–43, down from 45–38 before the election.

The secret to Senator Boxer's success in previous campaigns had been due in large part to the fact that she was an early adopter of the "war on women" strategy. Over the years, she had skillfully used wedge issues like abortion to compensate for the fact that she had, after almost thirty years in Washington, no positive record to run on. The strategy she had employed so effectively against her male opponents in the past didn't work against me in 2010. Pundits were hailing it as the "Year of the Republican Woman" in California thanks to Meg Whitman's and my victories. Two women at the top of the GOP ticket forced Senator Boxer to switch from the gender card to the class card. No sooner had the votes been counted in the primary than she pronounced me a "heartless" businesswoman who had eliminated and outsourced thousands of jobs while taking millions of dollars for myself at Hewlett-Packard. And for the next six months, Boxer rarely missed the opportunity to play class warfare with my record.

My mantra on the campaign trail in 2010 was that in

*Shira Toeplitz, "Boxer's Monster Haul Dwarfs Fiorina," *Politico*, July 15, 2010.

the twenty-first century, any job could go anywhere. That meant that California had to fight for every job, because Texas, Arizona, North Carolina, India, Guatemala, and China were fighting for our jobs. Instead of fighting for jobs—instead of creating a climate where businesses would choose to locate and invest; instead of creating an educational system that prepared workers to thrive in a changing economy—the men and women who called themselves our leaders were actively driving away jobs and shortchanging education. The result was predictable: we had 12.6 percent unemployment in California. More than two million Californians were out of work, and hundreds of thousands more had simply quit looking for jobs. What added insult to injury was that, as private-sector jobs went missing, public-sector jobs were thriving. Government was feasting off the carcass of the American economy.

"The fact that Barbara Boxer attacks me for outsourcing jobs demonstrates that she has no idea what is going on in the twenty-first-century economy," I said. "That's why we need someone in Washington, D.C., who understands why jobs go and how to get them back."*

When jobs leave a community, the impact on people and families is devastating. Laying off someone is the toughest decision a business leader ever makes. Layoffs are always a last resort. And moving production isn't

*Maeve Reston, "Fiorina Says Her Experience Prepares Her for the Senate," *Los Angeles Times*, June 24, 2010.

easy either. There are always costs, disruptions, and delays that accompany such a decision. The easiest thing in the world is for politicians to demonize businesspeople. Most businesspeople, however, are geared to grow, rather than shrink, their business. Growth means success: more revenue, more profits, more customers, and more jobs. And disruption isn't good for business. Usually, behind a difficult decision to downsize or move is a set of circumstances that have made business growth or business survival in a particular community impossible. Sometimes, these are business failures. All too frequently, however, they are policy failures. When we make it too difficult to grow a business (as Obamacare has done) or to stay in business (as too many EPA regulations have done), it is politicians who need to look in the mirror. When politicians simply refuse to approve a project like the Keystone XL pipeline, while knowing that it will create jobs and be better for our environment than our current practice of shipping crude by rail, the demonization of businesspeople rings a little hollow.

Boxer had a much lighter lift when it came to jobs. In the few times she showed up to address the issue, she toured the state in a kind of victory tour, touting her enthusiastic support for the $862 billion Obama stimulus bill. At each stop, she stood with local Democratic leaders and union supporters to showcase mostly government infrastructure projects paid for with stimulus dollars. Her message, despite the steadily climbing jobless rate, was that the stimulus was somehow working. At stop after stop, she spun a fantasy tale of government spending in the stimulus that magically both created jobs *and* saved the planet. In her worldview, there was no problem government bureaucracy couldn't fix.

In contrast, I didn't have the luxury of pointing to a sugar daddy in Washington, D.C., who was going to save us. Instead, I formulated a jobs plan that included tax breaks for small businesses and special zones to attract manufacturing businesses with tax breaks and regulatory relief. The message, again, was that California had to fight for each and every job; my plan would do that. For a while, I seemed to get some traction with the public. The polls started to tighten.

In a state with more than seventeen million registered voters, 64 percent of California voters are either registered Democrats or independents. As summer ended with the race deadlocked, the California press began to ask why I wasn't following the usual political playbook and tacking to the left for the general election. One after another, the media ran with stories about how I was maintaining my conservative principles on abortion, marriage, energy, and the Second Amendment. No doubt, they were quick to add, I would be punished by Californians in a few weeks at the ballot box. They called my refusal to change my views a "risky strategy," a "fatal error." Even Chuck Devore declared himself "pleasantly delighted" that I hadn't run to the left.

Maybe I was naive, but I was betting that the voters cared more about the fact that unemployment was 12 percent and the national debt was $13 trillion (it's over $18 trillion today) than they did about any other single issue. I was betting that the voters were prepared to find common ground with a candidate who was open and empathetic with them even if we didn't agree on every issue. My experience in business had taught me that the way you get a deal made is to know what your principles are—to know exactly what red lines you won't cross—and then be prepared to collaborate elsewhere to find common ground. I knew and respected the fact that I didn't agree with lots of Californians on the sanctity of life, for example. I also knew, given the chance, we could find common ground on issues like sex-selective abortion and late-term abortion. So I took the risk; I made the bet. In the end, I didn't have any choice. My beliefs weren't poll tested. I am who I am.

■ ■ ■

For the people of California, the final weeks of campaign 2010 were a relentless barrage of campaign commercials. Meg Whitman and Jerry Brown were battling it out for governor on the airwaves, and Californians were growing weary of all the political noise. Then, in mid-September, Barbara Boxer added to the noise with a blistering ad campaign attacking me. As she had before, she kept her focus on distorting and discrediting my record at Hewlett-Packard.

The ads were relentlessly negative and distorting, but they were a departure from Boxer's previous campaigns. The press began to wonder aloud when she would revert to form and reach into her tried and true bag of gender wedge issues. We didn't have long to wait. On October 15, Senator Boxer appeared at a press conference at the Roosevelt Hotel in Hollywood with a gaggle of actresses, pro-abortion groups, and congressional liberals to condemn my view on life. She declared in her usual hyperbole that "a woman's right to choose is on the ballot here in California this year." For the remainder of the campaign she continually accused me of having, in her words, "Sarah Palin values." It was her attempt to change the subject, and it worked. With less than three weeks to go until election day, Boxer opened up an 8-point lead.

I was determined to run through the tape, and my team fought like champions. In early October we received a much-needed infusion of cash from the National Republican Senatorial Committee (NRSC), which allowed us to put up a statewide television ad calling out Senator Boxer's record (or lack thereof) on the economy. The NRSC chairman, Senator John Cornyn, came out to California for me multiple times. Senators Mitch McConnell, Lindsey Graham, John McCain, Saxby Chambliss, and John Thune made the long trip from Washington to California to support me. Some questioned why we continued to focus our ads on Boxer instead of doing more to introduce me to the electorate. In retrospect, it seems a fair criticism. Boxer's ads were defining me as a heartless job killer, and I didn't do enough to push back on that portrayal.

I had managed HP through a tumultuous time in the technology industry. I came in at the peak of the dot-com bubble and managed through the worst technology recession in twenty-five years. I inherited a bloated, sclerotic bureaucracy with too many people in "administration" and not enough in customer service. My mandate was to transform a company that had become a laggard and make it into a leader that could prosper and grow. In that we succeeded, although tough choices and difficult decisions were unavoidable. Although some people, regrettably, lost their jobs, many more jobs were created. Only growth, success, and leadership can guarantee prosperity. It is true of companies, and it is true of countries as well.

Our days on the campaign trail, in the meantime, were punishing. We did three events in three different towns a day and then usually a smaller fund-raising gathering every night. Our focus on the stump, as ever, was jobs, jobs, jobs. One typical day on the campaign trail involved a morning visit to a pizza business that was being forced to lay off workers. Then a midday stop at an online consumer credit services company that was being forced to locate outside of California. Finally, that afternoon, an event featuring an electrical contractor who hadn't taken a salary in four and a half months.

Days like that can take a toll on even the strongest of people. Although it had been more than a year since I had completed treatment and was declared cancer free, I was still living, as so many women do, with repairing my body from the effects of cancer treatment. On October 25, after another grueling day of campaigning, I got back to my hotel room late, feeling terrible. Around five a.m. I knew I was in trouble; my entire left side was on fire. I texted my surgeon, who had also become my friend, Dr. Lauren Greenberg, and asked whether I should go to the hospital. Her immediate answer: "Absolutely." I woke Frank and called Deborah, who was also traveling with us. Early that morning, with exactly one week to go until election day, I checked into UCLA hospital.

After the nightmare I went through during the primary, I had had breast reconstruction surgery that summer. The implant in my left breast had become infected. To prevent the spread of infection, the doctor would have to remove the implant surgically and clean out the incision. Deborah later told me she worried that I was slipping away as I went into surgery. The last thing I remember is the nurse taking my temperature. It was 107 degrees.

Against the wishes of my doctors, I insisted on being released the day after surgery, on Wednesday, with six days to go until the election. The condition was that we work out a complicated process for me to receive an aggressive schedule of antibiotics. We all put on a brave face, but something had shifted. With the perspective of time, it's clear that I was very ill. I think Deborah, Marty, Julie, and the team saw that. Everyone continued to work as hard and as heroically as ever, but something had changed.

In those final days, the national Democratic machine cranked up to full capacity to reelect Barbara Boxer. President Obama came out for a fund-raiser and a rally. Michelle Obama followed a few days later. The vice president and Mrs. Biden came out. Cabinet members appeared at last-minute get-out-the-vote events. The last polls of the race that Friday showed her maintaining an 8-point lead.

The Sunday before the election, Frank and I went to see Stu Spencer, Ronald Reagan's campaign manager, and his wife, Barb. His daughter, Karen, who was a faithful friend and adviser throughout the campaign, had introduced us. Stu had generously offered his counsel and support. We sat at brunch and he told me how he had been looking at the polls. Things were tough, he said, but I could still win. And then he asked what seemed to me to be a strange question: "What's the weather going to be like on Tuesday?" "It's supposed to be beautiful," I answered. "Well then," he said with a completely serious face, "you will lose. The other side will drive around L.A., hand out bottles of whatever they need to, and get people to the polls." Frank and I left that meeting grateful for Stu's wisdom and friendship but dejected by his assessment.

Election night was frustratingly anticlimactic. Going in we knew the absentee ballots were trending our way. As the night went on and the returns showed Boxer in the lead, we held out hope. Then, before the results could come in from L.A. County, home to more than one in four registered voters, the California secretary of state's Web site went down. Nonetheless, they called the election for Boxer. We put off conceding the race. The absentee ballots were still out, and the Web site was still down.

As the night wore on, Senator Boxer delivered her victory speech, but we remained in limbo. My supporters were gathering at our election night headquarters, and it was getting late. I had to say something to them, but the question was, what? It was frustrating to come to this point, with family, friends, and well-wishers all around me and not know what to tell them. That, and I was tired. Tired from relentless campaigning. Tired of fighting with my uncooperative body to heal. Before I went out to speak, I went into the bathroom and ripped out the drains the doctors had put in me the week before. I adjusted my suit and walked out. Frank knew what I had done. "Those weren't supposed to come out for another few days," he said. "What are you doing?" I wasn't sure, but I did know this: I had to go speak to my supporters—

most likely for the last time. I would be damned if I was going to do it with those pieces of plastic in my body.

Then I walked out onto an empty stage to address the crowd. Despite the uncertainty that hung in the air, the crowd cheered. A wave of Republican victories was sweeping the nation that night. There was reason to cheer.

"It's a great night to be a Republican," I told the crowd. "But California is always a little bit different." They laughed. I wasn't there to concede the race, I said. The fact was we still didn't know who had won and who had lost. I encouraged my supporters to go home, and Frank and I returned to our hotel. At 12:30 that night the secretary of state's Web site came back up. We had been flooded in L.A. County. The race was over. We had lost.

I woke up the next morning knowing exactly what I had to do. Frank looked at me and said, "You're really okay, aren't you?" And it was true. I was okay. We had made mistakes, but I was proud of the race we had run. I called Senator Boxer to congratulate her. Then I faced the cameras for the last time as a candidate. The numbers were in, but the issues we had raised in our campaign had not changed. Too many lives and livelihoods were being destroyed. Too much human potential was being crushed.

"The fight is not over. The fight has just begun," I said. And then we went home.

CHAPTER 6

A Cautionary Tale

THERE IS A DAY AFTER THE SENATE RACE THAT stands out in my mind. We had come to Virginia for Christmas as we usually did. It was a bright, beautiful December day. Kara, Morgan, and I were in Georgetown. We were Christmas shopping. I remember crossing the street, hand in hand with my girls. It was warm and sunny, and we were having fun. I remember thinking to myself: this is a good life. I had no sense of regret, only great blessings. It was a moment of grace.

In a life full of ebbs and flows, it was a time of clarity and transition. Life was flowing. Frank and I missed being with Tracy, Lowell, Kara, and Morgan. We began to think of moving back home to Virginia, where we had first met, married, and bought our first home. I love looking at houses, so I went on the Internet. I found a wonderful house on the banks of the Potomac in Mason Neck, Virginia—close to George Mason's home, Gunston Hall, and about ten miles south of George Washington's home, Mount Vernon. We drove out to see it and instantly fell in love, although we couldn't come to terms with the seller. We had lots of time, so we spent the first part of 2011 in California. There was no need to rush. We finally closed on the house in early summer, and by October we had moved back home to Virginia.

Leaving California was very difficult for me. California was where I spent most of my childhood. It was the place where my father had been a judge. It is the state whose beauty and character my mother had captured on canvas. I had gone to college there and led an iconic Golden State company. California is in my veins and always will be.

California is also a cautionary tale for America. Theodore Roosevelt once said that California is "west of the West." What he meant was that California was America at its youngest and most full of potential—the land of opportunity in a nation of opportunity. That was the California in which Bill Hewlett and Dave Packard created the largest technology company in the world from the garage behind Dave Packard's house. That same alchemy of wide-open opportunity, brains, and grit that gave birth to Hewlett-Packard also produced Intel,

Apple, Google, eBay, and thousands of other great companies.

The California of HP and Google is still with us; fortunes can still be made and the future shaped in Silicon Valley. What has changed—drastically—is the California of the middle and working classes. That was the California of Ronald Reagan, a place where schoolteachers and policemen and aerospace workers with families could afford to own a home and a yard. The public schools worked. The weather kept energy bills low. And the same income and education that would only cover a rented apartment back East could get a house in a quiet neighborhood. In California.

And so they came: the middle class, the destitute, visionaries seeking their fortunes, and exiles seeking a home. Many of the Okies who fled the great Dust Bowl in the 1930s settled in California's San Joaquin Valley. In the Central Valley, Americans with little besides strong backs and a work ethic could make a life for themselves and their families. These Americans came from all over America and, later, from all over the world. Devin Nunes, who today represents the southern Central Valley in the U.S. Congress, is a descendant of such immigrants. His people came from Portugal decades ago to live and work in the San Joaquin Valley. For Congressman Nunes, who has fought long and hard to restore the water flow to the parched and dying farms of the Central Valley, there is a bitter irony to the decline of the middle and working classes in California. The great-great-grandchildren of the Dust Bowl refugees, he laments, are being forced to live in another dust bowl, one created by the federal government.

I spent so much of my time during the 2010 campaign visiting with and talking about the people of the Central Valley because it is their experience that best illustrates how California has changed for ordinary Americans. They came to live the American Dream. But what was possible for Californians of earlier generations is no longer possible for Californians of today. The people haven't changed. The dream isn't dead. What's gone is the leadership that allowed the dream to flourish.

■ ■ ■

Much has been written about how California has become a hostile environment for business, particularly small businesses. *Chief Executive* magazine has named California the worst state in America for doing business, not once, not twice, but for nine years and counting. For those who shrug off such surveys as self-interested pro-business propaganda (another 2011 poll of California business groups reported that 82 percent of owners and executives said if they weren't already located in California they wouldn't consider going into business there), the details of what has been called the great California exodus should remove any doubt.

Businesses are leaving California. The list of companies picking up and moving to less-expensive places to do business reads like the Dow Jones index. In 2014 Toyota sent a clear message to Sacramento when it announced it was moving its headquarters from Torrance to Plano, Texas. Toyota's move follows a procession of high-profile departures in recent years, including Nissan, Raytheon, Occidental Petroleum, fast-food operator CKE Restaurants (it takes two years to open a new restaurant in California today), eBay, Google, and McAfee—and these are just the most recognizable names. A business consultant who tracks departures from the Golden State counted over 250 businesses with more than 100 employees that left or expanded someplace other than California in 2011. The business climate has only gotten worse since then. Surveys consistently give California bad grades when it comes to small businesses as well. The *Economist* quoted a longtime observer who described the state of California's consistent message to business as this: "F___ you, f___ you, f___ you, f___ you, f___ you, f___ you, f___ you, f___ you and f___ you."*

More important—and not coincidentally—people are leaving California too. The state was once a magnet—California added enough residents from other states between 1960 and 1990 to populate the entire state of Missouri. Then the flow of Americans to California re-

---

*The *Economist*, "The Not So Golden State," January 25, 2014.

―――

versed. For a time, foreign immigration made up for the loss, but since 2005 that, too, has slowed. Today, California's net migration is negative—more people leave than come to the state.* Critically, according to demographer Joel Kotkin, most of the people leaving California are ages five to fourteen and thirty-four to forty-five. It is young families who no longer see a future for themselves in California.

Why are middle-class families fleeing the Golden State? Real estate prices are high as a result of onerous antidevelopment regulations. Home ownership is simply out of reach for the middle class anywhere that doesn't require a lengthy commute through hellish traffic. And gas prices are high thanks to the highest gas tax in the country. New environmental regulations promise to drive them even higher. Environmental regulations are also driving up energy costs—electricity is already 50 percent more expensive in California than the national average—and driving out good manufacturing jobs. Of the more than 10,000 industrial facilities built or expanded in America between 2007 and 2010, only 176 were in California. Put differently, the state with 12 percent of the nation's population built 1.6 percent of the new industrial capacity.†

Add to that the highest personal income taxes in the

---

*Tom Gray and Robert Scardamalia, "The Great California Exodus," Manhattan Institute Report, September, 2012.

†Richard Rider, "Unaffordable California," California Policy Center, December 29, 2014. http://californiapolicycenter.org/unaffordable-california-it-doesnt-have-to-be-this-way-4/.

country, and California isn't such a good deal for the middle class anymore. In fact, it's a very bad deal. And what makes the state the canary in a coal mine for other states is that it's a bad deal created by government. Decisions made by politicians and bureaucrats are driving middle-class families to the exits.

Some argue that many Americans don't mind paying more in taxes to get more from government in return. After all, as liberal former representative Barney Frank famously said, "Government is simply the name we give to the things we choose to do together." Putting aside, for a moment, how much choice is involved, there is some truth to the notion that Americans will remain in high-tax states if they feel they are getting something in return. Writing in the *City Journal*, political scientist William Voegeli argues that a state can get away with high taxes if it offers its residents commensurately high services. California, however, is failing to make good on this promise. Californians pay high taxes, but they don't buy middle-class families very much.

Californians pay steep and growing taxes on gas, but the state has the fourth worst highways. California's public schoolteachers are the fourth highest paid, but California students rank forty-eighth in math and forty-ninth in reading.* Taxpayers subsidize mandated alternative

---

*Richard Rider, "Unaffordable California," California Policy Center, December 29, 2014. http://californiapolicycenter.org/unaffordable-california-it-doesnt-have-to-be-this-way-4/.

energy projects and get higher electricity costs in return. All in all, when compared with a state like Texas, less of California's state spending goes to things that will benefit the middle class—like roads and schools—and more toward things that benefit government itself, like pensions and health care plans.

In other words, government has gotten so big and so powerful in California that it's begun to work for itself. It's not a mysterious phenomenon—it's an entirely predictable one. And it has lessons for the rest of the country.

I've been around a lot of bureaucracies, both in business and in government. All bureaucracies have some common characteristics. They are rules-based, process-driven, hierarchical organizations. They do not reward creativity or innovation or judgment. They crush the potential of even good employees because, in a bureaucracy, people quickly get the message: follow the rules, don't rock the boat, send it up the line. Vast bureaucracies are not efficient. They are not effective. They don't change easily.

What's worse, over time, bureaucracies start to focus on power and self-preservation. They begin to forget why they were created and who they are supposed to serve. In business, bureaucracies forget customers. In government, they forget veterans, schoolchildren, commuters, home owners, seniors. Taxpayers.

This is the story of California. It is the story of government bureaucracy owing its survival to the taxpayers but pledging allegiance to itself. At the same time, of course, this vast bureaucracy is doing things. It's churning out rules and regulations and processes. It's enforcing the rules, regulations, and processes it already has. What is a good day at the office for a bureaucrat other than a day in which he acts successfully on behalf of the rules that define his existence? His power is inversely related to the power of the citizens whose lives and livelihoods he commands. And the power of the union bosses who control his fate—and thus, indirectly, the fate of the citizenry—is greater still.

In an environment like this, big business can survive if it chooses to. It has the armies of lawyers, lobbyists, and accountants it takes to navigate the obstacles erected by the state. It's small business and the middle class that wither under the assault. And not only can't small businesses keep up with the cost of taxation and regulation, larger companies move middle-class jobs elsewhere when they can. Silicon Valley may continue to produce new technology companies, but once the start-up phase is over, they typically move production and manufacturing jobs elsewhere. A small number of highly compensated research and development jobs remain, but good middle-class jobs are forced out.

Americans of all political persuasions, but particularly liberal populists like Elizabeth Warren who lament the gap between the rich and the poor, should take note. California has the fastest rising income inequality in the country. Even the liberal Center of Budget and Policy Priorities said California had the third worst income inequality in the nation from 2008 to 2010.* As the middle class is driven out, California's population increasingly comes to resemble a barbell, with the very rich on one end and the very poor on the other. California is now the home of 111 billionaires, with assets greater than the entire gross domestic product of all but twenty-four countries in the world. It is also home to the highest poverty rate in the country. In between, the middle class that survives is largely composed of government employees— the very bureaucrats who have milked the middle class of the private economy into virtual extinction.

■ ■ ■

To give credit where credit is due, California's problems aren't entirely lost on its leaders. Recent administrations have made modest attempts at reform. Some of these modest reforms have survived the Democratic-controlled legislature, albeit in an even more watered-down form. Taxes have been raised. Some politicians, not the least of whom is Democratic governor Jerry Brown, have even suggested that California has made a "comeback." Even though the state continues to have an unsustainable pub-

*Troy Senik, "Land of Inequality," *National Review,* March 10, 2014.

lic pension debt, the bureaucrats in Sacramento, for the time being at least, are taking in more than they are currently spending.

But one Californian's comeback is another Californian's continued misery. It is certainly true that for the state's power elites—what Joel Kotkin calls the gentry liberals—things are great in California. Opportunity is plentiful. Money is no object. They have no use for the public schools. Their property is protected by regulations that prevent encroachment by the less wealthy. Their politics are reflected in the social and environmental directives coming out of Sacramento.

It's not that these elites are bad people. They're concerned about the environment and about the poor and disenfranchised—I take them at their word on that. But they and other liberals have come to believe that their concerns and their solutions—their ideology—are more important than others' lives and livelihoods. The liberal impulse is well intentioned, but it is ultimately callous and disrespectful to the very people it is intended to help. It's message—whether liberals realize it or not—is this: we're smarter than you. So it's okay if we destroy your livelihood or limit your life. We'll take care of you.

Liberals often use compassion as the excuse to sacrifice others on the altar of their ideology; it is for the greater good, they say. But eventually, this rationalization is exposed as simple arrogance. MIT economist Jonathan Gruber's infamous statement about the passage of

Obamacare—that its authors had to lie about its effects due to the "stupidity of the American voter"—is an example of this. President Obama's unilateral move late in 2014 to change the immigration law with regard to millions of undocumented immigrants is another. Whether you agreed with the move or not, the point is that it didn't matter—not to President Obama. He knew better what was good for the country than the people he was elected to serve.

This callous disregard of the people's will is ruining California. It is also at the core of the philosophical political divide that confronts us as Americans. Years of experience in both business and public policy have taught me that the core difference between people is their belief—or lack of belief—in the capacity and potential of their fellow human beings. Our Founders bequeathed us a system that recognizes and honors the potential of every one of us to live a life of dignity and purpose. The difference between Americans—especially those who would lead us— is that some accept this premise and others don't.

As a conservative, I know that no one of us is better than another. I understand that any one of us may need a helping hand from time to time. But that doesn't mean my compassion for them or their compassion for me trumps our equal right to live a life of dignity and purpose. I may believe ardently in my ideology. However, that doesn't mean my ideology is more important than my fellow Americans' lives and livelihoods.

Many liberals feel differently. They mouth the words of equality, but they believe some people are smarter than others, and these people are entitled to decide for others. Mr. Gruber is just the most blatant example. Sometimes they are imposing their will out of what I'm sure they believe is a sincere concern for others. In other cases, such as the farmers in the San Joaquin Valley, they are simply sacrificing others' lives and livelihoods to their ideology. In both cases, this is the philosophy that, despite its good intentions, creates ever bigger government, nurtures ever more powerful bureaucracy, and crushes the potential of the people.

The same thing is happening in Kentucky to the coal miners, in Detroit to the small businesses, and in Bill de Blasio's New York to the parents desperate to send their children to a decent public school. Politicians and bureaucrats are putting their will over the needs of the people. When the head of the Chicago Teachers Union says that teachers can't be held responsible for their students' performance because so many children come from poor and broken homes, she's saying that these children don't have a future. Far from unlocking their potential, she's denying it.

Every woman aspiring to feed and clothe and care for her children is struggling to unlock her potential. When she learns that she might be trapped forever in a tangled web of programs that deepen her dependence over time, she does not believe hers is a life that matters to politicians. Good intentions or not, her potential will remain untapped.

■ ■ ■

I have been hard on California's leadership, but for good reason. For me and for many, many others, California has the potential to regain its footing as the place where American families come to achieve their dreams. It is still a beautiful place, awash in human and natural resources. Not only can California lead the nation in creativity and innovation, it has the potential to become, once again, a welcoming place for the middle class. It can be a place where strivers and exiles don't just chase—but achieve—the American Dream.

The lesson of California, like the lesson of New York City before it, is that ideas and policy matter. Most of all, leadership matters. If bureaucracies and radical ideology crush human potential, leadership unlocks it. If leaders can envision a different future for California, as Mayor Rudy Giuliani once envisioned for New York, they can make that vision a reality for its residents.

The same core choice that confronts California confronts America. In the Golden State's tragedy comes our opportunity to learn: in its travails is our cautionary tale. We face a choice. California shows us one path. There is another. It is the path toward a nation that once again lifts people up, extinguishes despair, and rekindles hope.

It is the path toward a nation in which all people fulfill their potential.

In 2011 I left California behind, but I have never forgotten its lessons. In the next several years would come the opportunity to share them with more of my fellow Americans. I confess I would not have predicted the reception I would receive.

CHAPTER 7

What Women Want

I WAS AT A CAMPAIGN EVENT IN NEW YORK IN 2014 when I finally put into words the disgust I have felt for our politics for a long time, particularly as they concern women. I was in New York City to support Rob Astorino, a local official who was mounting a bid to unseat Democratic governor Andrew Cuomo. It was an event for women who support Astorino. Cuomo shock troops posing as women's rights activists had targeted the event. They were out on the sidewalk, confronting the reporters and attendees. The protestors were there, they said, to demand that Rob sign a pledge to support the Women's Equality Act in the state legislature.

The Women's Equality Act. It was a nice title—who

isn't for women's equality? And nine out of its ten points had broad, bipartisan support in the New York legislature. It was the tenth point that was the poison pill. It would loosen New York law to permit abortion up to the ninth month of pregnancy by a nondoctor. It was the classic political setup, a tactic increasingly employed these days: wrap an extreme policy proposal in a benign-sounding title and dare your opponents to oppose it. When they do, use it in a thirty-second ad.

A reporter dutifully asked Rob if he supported the act. He said no, and began to explain why. It was at that point that I could no longer keep silent. I was sick of it. Sick of the games being played in our politics. Sick of the way the press and politicians know that games are being played, but no one questions it. Sick, especially, of the fact that at a time when people are losing their health insurance, real wages are falling and Americans are being beheaded by monsters in the Middle East, women are being manipulated by these kinds of campaign tricks. New York has among the worst economies and most corrupt politics in the nation. And here we were, playing games of political "gotcha."

I asked Rob if I could interject and tried to keep the frustration out of my voice. "One of the things that happens in politics a lot is people like to give something a name that sounds good, but the reality is something very different," I said. "The tenth point says that a woman can receive an abortion up to nine months from a nondoctor.

Really? This is supportive of women? This is inhumane to a woman and her child."

Then I got animated. "When New York is fifty out of fifty with the worst job climate, that doesn't help women," I said. "If anyone is waging a 'war on women,' it's the liberal policies that have produced a lack of opportunity in Cuomo's New York."

The gaggle of normally feisty New York reporters listening to my comments stopped. They were silent. Apparently no one else had ever bothered to question whether the Women's Equality Act was actually good for women. No one had ever punctured the balloon of politics as usual.

I had been around politics enough by that time, between the McCain campaign and my Senate run, to know that we needed to puncture more of these politics-as-usual balloons. Maybe it's because I come from outside that world, but there is a formula to what passes for our public debate that I find increasingly distasteful. It consists of partisan groups posing as independent advocates, setting traps for their opponents. The politicians they support then pay them off with their votes. And the people's voices, their lives, and livelihoods are shut out of the whole cynical, self-interested game. No one ever steps back and says, "Wait a second. Whose interests are actually being served here? What is this conversation really about—the people's business or the business of getting reelected?"

Americans have had enough of the games. After the president issued his unilateral change in the immigration law in 2014, I told a disbelieving Chuck Todd on *Meet the Press* that I believed the president's real aim was to goad congressional Republicans into a showdown—a confrontation that the president believed would damage their standing among Hispanics and enhance his. His talk is all about compassion for illegal immigrants, I said, but his actions exploit them for his own political gain. They are puppets in his cynical political play.

"He sunk comprehensive immigration reform in 2007," I said. "He did nothing to push forward immigration reform when he had the Senate, the House, and the White House. He said in '11 and '12 he couldn't do anything. And then he delayed his action for the elections. Unbelievable cynicism."

It's worth asking the question no one on *Meet the Press* bothered to ask: whose interests were really being served by the president's action? It did nothing to resolve the final status of illegal immigrants in America. Worse yet, it made the possibility of real immigration reform— reform that protects the borders and fixes our broken system—a virtual impossibility. The president didn't succeed in goading Congress into a showdown, but he did succeed in making members very angry. Immigrants in America, both legal and illegal, will pay the price.

The cynical games being played and the disconnect between political rhetoric and reality, it seems to me, are particularly acute when it comes to women. Women are half the nation. If jobs are scarce and wages are falling, women are suffering just as much as men. And if college is unaffordable, day care eats up an entire paycheck, and health insurance premiums are rising, women are most likely suffering *more* than men. It's women who balance the checkbooks and make the health care and education decisions. These aren't what politicos call women's issues, but they weigh on women all the same. And how does our political system answer that concern? With condescension. With phony controversies designed to win elections.

■ ■ ■

I was no stranger to how poorly served women are by our political process, of course. I had seen—and felt—firsthand the tactics employed by liberals like Barbara Boxer to keep her base among gender activists placated. I'd seen, as well, how my own party had failed women in various ways.

I met a woman at a Kansas event for Governor Sam Brownback. She was, she told me, a faithful Republican volunteer. Like so many other women in our party, she stuffed the envelopes, she manned the phone banks, walked the neighborhoods, and raised the money. She told me she was losing hope in her party. She was tired of doing the work while the hierarchy of the party took the credit. She encouraged me to continue speaking to men and women about our principles, our priorities, and our potential. I knew what she meant. So many women see the tableaux of smiling female faces behind the male officeholders and wonder why those smiling faces rarely seem to be asked to speak—unless, of course, it is a "women's event."

From my travels around the country, I've noticed that the GOP has two distinct but related problems with women voters. First, many GOP-leaning women are apathetic. They may have previously voted with Republicans, but they've become disenchanted or perhaps have just disengaged. Second, many women are open to voting for Republicans but have to be persuaded. Neither group much likes the tone and tenor of politics. They are put off by the vitriol, the arguing, the seemingly endless posturing, and the paucity of results. Women tend to be both doers and collaborators—their complicated, busy lives require both skill sets. They get frustrated when they don't see much of either in the political process.

This is a tragedy, because women—every bit as much as men, maybe more so—have the potential to contribute to our party. They are neither the helpless victims nor the unthinking drones nor the single-issue hysterics our politics treated them as. I know from being a CEO that any company needs as much talent around the table as it can possibly muster. Failing to take advantage of the talents of women—half the population—is corporate malpractice as far as I'm concerned. The same is true for any party that hopes to be a governing party. And the Republican Party must be as diverse as the nation we want to represent.

The question for me has always been how to reach American women at the grassroots. In 2010, following my Senate race, I got involved with a group called the American Conservative Union (ACU). The ACU is a storied organization with great leaders and great ideas. I was interested in learning more about change from the bottom up in the conservative movement, so I joined the ACU board and later became chairman of the ACU Foundation.

As chairman of the foundation I've been working hard to communicate the power of conservative ideas to unlock the potential of all Americans. We've created policy centers with some of the brightest minds in the conservative movement to develop proactive, practical solutions and recommendations for the problems that confront our nation, including the role of government, citizenship education, poverty, national security, government spending, and criminal justice reform. We are talking to both policy makers in Washington as well as opinion leaders and voters beyond the Beltway. I'm convinced that the more Americans know about conservative principles and how they can improve our lives, the better the nation will be.

The ACU hosts a gathering each spring called the

Conservative Political Action Conference, or CPAC, which brings in grassroots conservatives from all corners of the country. Great conservative leaders, from Ronald Reagan to presidential contenders since the 1970s, have addressed CPAC. In the winter of 2014, I gave a speech to CPAC that unexpectedly launched me in a new adventure to give voice to more American women in our political process.

The 2014 midterm elections were under way at the time, and the airwaves were full of Democratic talk about the so-called Republican war on women. Desperate to change the subject from the rise of ISIS, the disaster of Obamacare, and the president's low approval ratings, liberals were engaged in what I found to be a naked attempt at manipulating American women. They were treating us like children, and not very bright children at that.

Conservatives are different, I told the group. "We respect all women and don't insult them by thinking that all they care about are reproductive rights. All issues are women's issues," I said. "We are half of this great nation." The audience cheered their approval.

"Women balance the checkbooks. That's why women care that we can't balance the checkbook in Washington, D.C. Women make the health care and education decisions for our families. Women worry about our own jobs, our children's futures, and our husbands' jobs."

The object was to paint conservatives as cold and uncaring. We have to fight that, I said, not just by pushing back against the phony "war on women," but by our own words and deeds.

"Ask struggling single moms what they need," I said. "They need our help. And while we know that God gave each of them dignity and self-respect, they need those things from us too. And they need and deserve a job. They need leadership to unlock their potential."

The audience was on their feet by the time I had finished. Immediately after the speech I had a media interview. As I moved through the convention center, I was accosted by young people—mostly young women—who told me they loved the speech and asked me to keep talking about the issues I had raised. Most men were reluctant to take on the "war on women" tactic, they said. They knew it was another political game designed to discredit what they believe and that the media was playing right along. They were eager for someone to expose it and to puncture the political balloon.

I didn't have to think about it long. There was no "war on women," but there was a range of issues, from jobs to health care to security, on which women were eager to engage. I began to envision an organization that would target women at the grassroots with the tools and opportunity to make their voices heard. I wasn't interested in engaging women the way the Democrats were, as an identity group with certain narrow concerns. I wanted to reach out to women because we are half of the nation.

Real change will not occur unless we are part of it. I immediately set about raising money, and in June we unveiled the Unlocking Potential Project (UP).

I spent the next six months traveling to our target states—Colorado, Iowa, New Hampshire, North Carolina, and Virginia. We chose purple states, swing states that were neither predominantly Republican nor predominantly Democratic. I spent days in classrooms, conference rooms, and small auditoriums conducting training sessions with interested women. We know that women are most persuaded by women they know. We also know that the issues that matter most to women, contrary to the claims of the left, are the economy, government spending, and health care. The idea was to motivate them and educate them to get other women involved in the electoral process. So we armed our UP trainees with data with which to make the case to women they know to get out and vote. Instead of just focusing on reproductive issues, we talked about the record number of women in poverty, how women are losing access to health care, and how wages are falling.

In our sessions we would "unpack" some of the myths about women and conservatives' attitudes toward them. For example, the issue of equal pay. Despite the impression the New York activists were trying to create with the Women's Equality Act, conservatives and Republicans support equal pay for equal work. Equal pay for equal work became the law of the land in 1963. Any woman who is discriminated against in her paycheck simply because she is a woman should take advantage of all the legal recourse she has at her disposal. The biggest obstacle to women earning as much as men, I told UP audiences, is the seniority system. The seniority system rewards time in grade and not merit or performance. And because women are so often the last hired and the first fired, it is harder for them to achieve time in grade. And who supports the seniority system? Union and government bureaucracies. Democrats may play games with things like the Women's Equality Act, but for them union bureaucracies are serious political business. They support them down the line, and in doing so, continue to support unequal pay for equal work.

Instead of falling for the traps of the "war on women," we trained our volunteers to steer their political conversations toward the facts of women in the economy today. Fact: since 2008 almost four million women have fallen into poverty. Fact: since 2008 women have seen their annual median income decline by $733. Fact: the labor force participation rate for women is at a new all-time low of 56 percent.

After spending several hours digesting the data and role-playing the conversations they would have, we gave our volunteers lists of persuadable women and charged them with finding five women to join them in the movement. Each of these women would, in turn, engage fifteen other women. Our targets were politically unaffiliated women who are persuadable and registered Republicans who didn't often come out to vote.

What we learned in the Unlocking Potential Project is that women—particularly women struggling to raise families alone—are uniquely suffering under the weight of the bureaucratic state. At one UP event in New Hampshire, a woman told her story. She and her husband were lawyers with a law practice in Boston. When her husband died unexpectedly, she took her small children and moved to New Hampshire. She decided to open up her own small law practice in New Hampshire so she could be home with her kids while at the same time supporting her family. Then Obamacare came along and she lost her insurance policy. The only new plan she could get under the law didn't allow access to her children's pediatrician or the family grief counselor. Unable to afford the premiums or the deductible, she was forced to give up on her business and go to work for a big law firm. Now she's working more hours and bringing home less money. She can't be there for her children, she told us, and she still doesn't have access to the family doctors they once counted on.

It was a wrenching story of a life hijacked by the very government that said it was trying to help her. This woman's entire life was being dictated to her by anonymous bureaucrats in Washington, D.C., accountable to no one, elected by no one. They not only held this woman's life in their hands, they had made it immeasurably worse.

Another lesson I learned from UP is that American women yearn for real conversation about real issues. Every issue that matters to the nation matters to them. They have real points of view on some of them and are willing to admit they need to learn more about others. Persuasive conversations take time and people to have them, and so we set out to find community captains who could have these interactions with women where they lived, worked, and worshipped. I am tremendously grateful to the 86 captains, our over 250 volunteers, and our 105 advisers who guided our on-the-ground efforts. They held training events, roundtables, and small group gatherings in our targeted states. All in all, we had conversations with over 60,000 voters.*

I learned that women are also very savvy users of social media. They are most persuaded by other women they know—whether face-to-face or virtually. And so we engaged with around 140,000 voters through online social media such as Facebook and Twitter.

Finally, what I learned is this: women can be a potent force in politics. They represent untapped potential. They are a force for positive change that neither political party has effectively leveraged. And in a relatively short amount of time, with very little money, we have demonstrated that women can make a difference in who we send to Washington, not because they are single-issue voters but because we care about all the issues.

In the end, the "war on women" tactic failed in 2014. In

crucial states like Colorado, women rejected the hysterical claims made by Democrats that Republicans would take away their birth control. It turns out that women want something more substantive from our political debate than phony controversies and campaign tricks. The question going forward is whether we will actually get it—and from whom.

■ ■ ■

Women in America may remain an underutilized resource, but women around the world are beyond underutilized. In too many places, they are subjugated as well.

In 2008, in partnership with Secretary of State Condoleezza Rice, I founded the One Woman Initiative to engage women in these countries. Both Secretary Rice and I had also been moved to act by the assassination of former Pakistani prime minister Benazir Bhutto a few months earlier. Women in countries like Pakistan, Egypt, India, and the Philippines, we believed, were the key to transforming those societies, not just economically but politically. Through the One Woman Initiative we gave them access to legal resources in cases of domestic violence, economic assistance for small businesses and farms, and training for greater political participation. Altogether we raised $100 million for projects to help the women who needed help most.

The philosophy behind the One Women Initiative was that empowering a single woman has unique ripple effects, not just in her family but in her community as well. She becomes, in effect, a leader. I have always believed that leaders are made, not born. I am a founding member of the African Leadership Academy, a school outside Johannesburg, South Africa, that teaches leadership. I traveled there a few years ago and was overwhelmed by what I saw: formerly impoverished and powerless young people, now in a place where someone was taking a chance on them. Each and every one of them had that look in their eyes—the opposite of the look of the men in Mendota. It is the look that says, I'm where I never thought I would be, and I'm doing something I never thought I was capable of doing. They were lit up from the inside.

The One Woman Initiative allowed me to see that look on the faces of some of the most powerless women in the world. A few years earlier I had become involved with another group, called Opportunity International, the largest microfinance organization in the world. Opportunity International promotes entrepreneurship—primarily female entrepreneurship, as it happens—by providing loans and other assistance to people with the least access to credit, savings, and other financial tools. In 2013 I decided to merge the One Women Initiative with Opportunity International. In 2014 I became the global chairman of the board of Opportunity. I am pleased to work alongside our outstanding global CEO, Vicki Escarra, and our tremendously dedicated board members, who, like me, donate their time, talent, and treasure. Although Opportunity is a nonprofit organization, we run it like a business. We want the accountability and effectiveness of business so that we can be wise stewards of both our donors' generosity and our clients' assets.

In a philanthropic landscape littered with Web sites designed to tug on heart strings and generate cash, Opportunity stands out for the work it is doing on the ground in some of the world's poorest countries. Opportunity is in twenty-two countries across the globe, providing small loans to mostly women entrepreneurs to start farms, small businesses, and, critically, schools. In Africa, most schools are run by proprietors who charge a fee to students to attend. Opportunity International not only provides a program called Edusave, which helps parents save for school for their children, it also helps fund schools with loans to operators.

Another way that Opportunity International stands out is that its operations are staffed and run by local people. They not only provide microloans, but also provide insurance, savings accounts, and mentors to female entrepreneurs. I have watched time and again how, through this work, nothing less than a miracle occurs. Women with no collateral or financial means take a small loan and build an enterprise that allows them to sell a product, employ others, and eventually save enough to send their children to school. Through a small loan, the cycle of poverty is broken. Not just families but entire communities are lifted by this miracle.

In Opportunity International I saw everything I had always believed about Americans reflected in women across the globe. What's true here at home is true in Congo, Tanzania, Romania, India, the Philippines, Columbia, and Nicaragua: the poor aren't poor because they lack ambition or intellect but because they lack opportunity, tools, and someone to take a chance on them. A job, an education—these things unlock potential and change lives. Opportunity International has changed millions of lives by loaning $8 billion over the past forty years—about $150 at a time.

Of all the miracles I've witnessed working with Opportunity International, few have moved me more than the story of Remy and Amina, a mother and daughter from the Philippines. Together, these women told their remarkable story to a hushed crowd of more than three hundred at Opportunity International's annual meeting in Chicago in 2014.

Remy began the story. She was nervous, and her English was halting. Still, she held the room transfixed. She had been a farmworker in a small village, earning two dollars a day through backbreaking work in the fields. Her husband earned just one dollar a day driving a motorcycle taxi. It was a daily struggle just to put food on the table at night. She never knew what they would eat or whether they would eat the next day and the day after that.

Remy wanted more for her two daughters. When she heard about Opportunity International, she took a $115 loan and bought three piglets. She began to earn money and reinvested it in her business. She bought a sow so she no longer had to buy piglets. She invested in a used sewing machine. Eventually, her piggery became a business that included selling vegetables, clothing, and rice. But she didn't have real success until she had earned enough to send her daughters to school. She had achieved something much larger than wealth. Her daughters were educated. "Our house is full of gold," she said. "We will not be hungry anymore."

When Remy's daughter rose to speak, it was clear how much Remy's sacrifice and investment had paid off. In flawless English, Amina spoke clearly, articulately, and lovingly about her parents' struggle and her family's transformation. She had been able to realize her dream of graduating from college. Now she had returned to the Philippines to work for OI. Someone—people she didn't know—had taken a chance on her.

"That was how I first understood how grace works," she said.

There wasn't a dry eye in the house. Remy and Amina had taken their first steps in preparing themselves to succeed in a new world full of change and opportunity.

CHAPTER 8

Unlocking America's Potential

THE WORLD IS A VERY COMPLICATED PLACE. Perhaps it has always has been, but I know this: the twenty-first century is a century unique in all of human history—unique in its complexity, in its dangers, and in its possibilities.

Like the strands of the DNA double helix, two forces intertwine and define our world today: technology and globalization. Each feeds and is accelerated by the other. Both are inexorable and unstoppable, in part because, despite all the disruption they cause, they also satisfy the basic human desire for lives of more opportunity and more control.

Around the year 2000, I gave a speech in which I defined the "next big thing" in technology. I called it DMVP: Digital, Mobile, Virtual, Personal. I theorized that everything physical and analog would, over time, become digital information; that information would be accessible on mobile devices; that virtual reality would become as compelling—and real—as physical reality; and people would have personal control over it all. This trend, I said at the time, would define our lives for the next twenty-five to thirty years. I have come to believe it will define our lives for as far as I can imagine.

We first became aware of this trend with music. We saw physical storage of analog music (think records) become physical storage of digital music (think CDs), and the stores that once sold them both, give way to bits and bytes delivered through an MP3 player. Within a few short years, an entire industry was transformed forever. The disruption was painful for some, profitable for others, empowering for many—but once begun, the process could not be stopped. Individuals who loved music preferred the access, the choice, and the control—not to mention the prices—that came with this new world.

Every industry is now being transformed by this unstoppable force. Education, health care, publishing, finance, retail . . . the list is endless. Every human endeavor from politics to art is being reshaped by Digital, Mobile, Virtual, Personal. We can think of examples both profane and profound. Fantasy football has become as compelling for many as the real thing. The global financial system and its regulators are starting to worry about how bitcoin, the most prominent of the virtual currency systems, will affect their world. Text messages and emojis are now the preferred form of communication and relationship for much of a generation.

The iPhone was introduced in 2007—less than a decade ago. Today we take for granted this revolutionary truth: for the first time in human history, anyone, anywhere can gain access to any piece of information they choose, or communicate with anyone they choose, at the time and place of their choosing, on any device. The amount of personal empowerment this grants an individual is astonishing. The ability to organize, galvanize, communicate, educate, and motivate—for good or for ill—is unprecedented. Our lives are changing before our eyes, and we have entered a new chapter in human history.

The Digital, Mobile, Virtual, Personal revolution is accelerating. We feel it in our everyday lives as the transformative power of technology—for better or for worse—changes everything around us at a faster and faster pace. And because information and communication of any type can move anywhere at breakneck speed, so can money, products, and jobs. The truth of this new century is that opportunity can go anywhere at any time.

Globalization is as inexorable a force as technology. Ours truly is a global economy. There are real and painful disruptions that come from this reality. And yet, it is in America's interests that others around the world have an opportunity to lift themselves out of poverty and take a stake in the world. Ours is a safer world when more people are more prosperous and when other nations have a real stake in our economy and vice versa. For example, while we watch China's new assertiveness with concern, and while we must be clear-eyed about their intentions, we also know that they are dependent on our markets and our products for their prosperity. Their dependence gives us leverage.

Exports have powered our economy in real ways that have provided real American jobs. Although there is no denying that globalization has destroyed some jobs in some American communities, there is also no denying that global trade creates opportunities for all nations, especially our own. And globalization cannot be stopped any more than the DMVP revolution can. People all over the world want an opportunity for a better life, just as people all over the world want an opportunity to be in control of as much of their lives as possible. This is human nature.

■ ■ ■

The combination of these two unstoppable forces has fundamentally altered America and the world in the twenty-first century. Technological change rewards speed, flexibility, and agility. Globalization means jobs and investment can go anywhere. The result is that competition is now global—and fierce—for every job and every dollar of investment. And not only do we have to compete for jobs, we have to compete for *good* jobs, and that means having a trained and educated workforce.

Most of all, in a world characterized by ceaseless change, constant disruption, grave dangers, and enormous possibilities, the most precious asset of all is human potential; the potential and the brainpower that creates the human capacity for invention, creativity, entrepreneurship, flexibility, and adaptability will determine who succeeds in this new world and who falls behind. Therefore the twenty-first century should be the American century, because this is the nation that has unlocked human potential better than any other nation on earth. The foundation of "life, liberty and the pursuit of happiness" has given people of imagination, energy, determination, and creativity the opportunity to pursue a better life for themselves and their families. The qualities that America has always celebrated are precisely the qualities we need most in this twenty-first-century world.

Why doesn't it feel like it's working out that way? A majority of Americans don't think their children's future will be better than their own. They believe their country is headed in the wrong direction. These views reflect a belief that we are not leading in this new century, but becoming victims of it. What's going on?

Remember the parable of California. Our nation faces a time of choosing. At a time when we most need speed, flexibility, entrepreneurship, innovation, derring-do, and can-do, a massive government bureaucracy sits atop our nation at every level—its weight crushing the very spirit that has always powered our economy and lifted our communities.

We are now, for the first time in American history, destroying more businesses than we are creating. More small businesses are dying than are being created for the first time since such data began to be collected.* Small businesses innovate at seven times the rate of big businesses, employ more than half of all Americans, and create over two thirds of new jobs. We cannot lift people out of poverty, rebuild the middle class, or lead in the twenty-first century unless we rebuild the entrepreneurial capacity of Main Street. When you ask small business owners why they are quitting, their answer is always the same: it's just too hard. Over 70 percent of small business owners describe the federal government as "hostile" toward them.†

We are no longer adequately educating our children. Although we have been spending more money on the Department of Education virtually every year for the past forty years, we continue to fall behind other nations in our educational outcomes. Whereas the advocates of

---

*Ian Hathaway and Robert E. Litan, "Declining Business Dynamism in the United States," Brookings Institution, May 2014.

†Kent Hoover, "Small Business Owners Upset by Lack of Spending Cuts in Fiscal Cliff Deal," bizjournals.com, January 15, 2013. http://www.bizjournals.com/bizjournals/washingtonbureau/2013/01/15/small-business-owners-upset-by-lack-of.html?page=all.

Common Core suppose that more centralized decision making is the answer, I would argue that the past forty years demonstrate beyond a shadow of a doubt that more money and more decision making at the national level have exacerbated our problems and cannot solve them. We need more variety in education, not more standardization. We need more choices for parents and children, and more control for them. We cannot let union bosses or bureaucrats determine whether a child can be educated. And so parents must have the ability to decide where and how their children are educated—whether it is at home, in parochial school, in a traditional public school, or in a charter school. Teachers and administrators must be held accountable by local communities. The single most important factor in a child's education is an involved parent and a great teacher. So we must encourage and reward both. Good teachers must be rewarded for their merit and poor teachers must focus on improving their performance—and there must be sufficient transparency that parents understand which teachers perform well and which do not. In other words, we need less central bureaucracy and more choice, more competition, and a focus on accountability and performance.

Proponents of Common Core argue that we must compete with the Chinese in subjects like math and science. I agree that we must compete, but we will not win by becoming more centralized and standardized in our education methods. Although the Chinese are a gifted people, innovation and entrepreneurship are not their strong suits. Their society, as well as their educational system, is too homogenized and controlled to encourage imagination and risk taking. Americans excel at such things, and we must continue to encourage them. A centralized bureaucracy in Washington shouldn't be telling teachers how to teach or students how to learn. Our states have been described as "laboratories of democracy." They are also laboratories of innovation.

More Americans are living in poverty, especially women and children. More Americans are facing lives of constrained choices and some degree of dependence. We have more and more government, more and more government spending, more and more government programs, more and more government bureaucracy—and less and less creativity, empowerment, and opportunity. Debt and deficits are spiraling out of control. The consequences for Americans in their neighborhoods are heartbreaking.

All of this is happening in a time when jobs and opportunity wait for no one. If we choose to crush our most precious assets—human potential and brainpower—under the weight of bureaucratic inertia, we will, over time, lose the ability to control our own destiny.

■   ■   ■

America's decline is neither necessary nor inevitable. Our wounds are all self-inflicted, our problems are all solvable, our potential and possibilities are as vast as they have ever been. We need different politics, different policies, and different leaders.

Politics has become the art of the sound bite. Some politicians blame this on the voters: it needs to be really simple so people can understand it, they say. I think most voters blame it on the politicians. Voters know the world is a complicated place and appreciate that sound bites won't suffice. What I think most voters want is an intelligent, respectful conversation about the real issues and the proposed solutions. They know that something has to change.

I learned long ago that complex challenges require systemic approaches. When faced with a complicated set of problems in a complicated environment, the "silver bullet"—the one simple solution that will change everything—doesn't exist. This is particularly true when the status quo has been in place for a long time. Those who have invested in the status quo and benefited from it are the most resistant to changing it. The power, the perks, and the prestige that come along with their positions within the system must be protected at all costs. And so real change always and literally requires the power of many people outside the status quo—people who have a vision for what can be achieved and a holistic, rather than piecemeal, approach for achieving it. There are many examples that illustrate this, but perhaps the most powerful of all is the story of our nation's founding.

When I was at Hewlett-Packard, I realized I needed a

model, a framework for thinking through an enormous set of complex challenges within a system that was becoming moribund. I wrote about this at great length in *Tough Choices*. The simple Leadership Framework that I crafted then has served me well in every situation since. And so it is the framework through which I analyze America's challenges today.

The Leadership Framework consists of four parameters—or literally, the four sides of a square:

Put another way, successful change requires a systemic approach that answers four basic kinds of questions:

What are we trying to achieve? What is our purpose?

How should we organize ourselves and our work to achieve these purposes?

> How will we measure our progress? How do
> we define and reward success?
>
> What do we value? What behavior do we
> encourage?

These are obviously interrelated questions and so all must be addressed. None can be ignored, or change will fail. This is systematic, holistic change that succeeds and endures.

Systemic change and a holistic vision of what is required do not imply a single, comprehensive solution to a long-standing problem. Indeed, successful change never occurs in one fell swoop. "Comprehensive immigration reform" will fail, just as comprehensive health care reform is failing. But to start a successful process of real reform—and to complete the change that is required—people need a road map. Where are we trying to go? How will we know when we have arrived? And then the journey begins, step by step, building confidence and consensus and capability along the way.

Goals and Strategy

Earlier in this book, I remarked that Americans agree on many things. Nowhere does this apply more than to the questions: What are we trying to achieve? What is our purpose?

On these questions, the answers are unambiguous and enjoy wide consensus.

We must unlock the potential of every single American, regardless of their circumstances. Doing so requires a helping hand when necessary, an education that equips one for the future, and a job.

We must revitalize Main Street so that small businesses can flourish once again. This requires a vastly simplified tax code and regulatory regime, the reemergence of community banks and community reinvestment programs, and a celebration of and support for the entrepreneurial spirit.

We must rebuild and retrain America. Our roads and our infrastructure are in terrible shape. The vaunted "stimulus" program spent much and achieved little. And as important as our roads and bridges are, of even greater concern is the number of able-bodied Americans who are no longer qualified for the jobs that exist. It is a tragedy that when manufacturing jobs open in many communities, there aren't enough qualified applicants to fill them while too many remain unemployed or underemployed. Although fixing our legal immigration system is a worthy and important goal, we should not have to look to India and China for adequately trained workers in certain industries. When someone is laid off at age fifty, we cannot discard them. We must retrain them so they can move on with their lives.

Obviously, we must fundamentally reform government. When the latest scandal at the Veterans Administration (involving the manipulation of wait times) broke into the public view, we all expressed outrage for the callous disregard with which our nation's heroes were treated. Equally shocking, however, and directly affecting the quality of care we are providing our veterans, is the reality that while Digital, Mobile, Virtual, Personal is transforming the rest of the world, the VA has been undergoing a major "systems upgrade" for over thirty years—since the 1980s. The agency's regional headquarters in Winston-Salem, North Carolina, was threatened recently because the weight of the paperwork piled high on bureaucrats' desks was damaging the buildings' foundations.* The rollout of the Affordable Care Act provided the best evidence for reform of all. The merits of Obamacare aside, how can a Web site costing hundreds of millions of dollars and several years of effort fail? Answer: because a series of government bureaucracies was in charge of building it.

The people of government are not incompetent. However, a large, ponderous bureaucracy, bound by rules, defined by hierarchy, is necessarily incompetent in the DMVP age. Bureaucracies literally cannot keep pace with the speed of change, the ubiquitous nature of information, or the complexity of the problems they are asked to solve. Bureaucracies were invented to maintain control.

---

*Mark Thompson, "Guess the VA *Does* Have a Paperwork Problem . . . ," *Time*, August 10, 2012.

The twenty-first century cannot be controlled. It can be leveraged and harnessed, but it cannot be controlled. Only ingenuity, flexibility, and creativity can prevail. And bureaucracies—by their nature—kill all these things. The liberals who argue that more government is the answer fail, most fundamentally, to realize this essential truth: bureaucracies cannot cope successfully in the new world in which we live. They will, under the best of circumstances, flail about. Under the worst of circumstances, they will inflict real damage.

We must restore American leadership in the global economy. We must be the economic powerhouse of the new century, and this means we must lead in energy production, in health care and the health sciences (including biotechnology), in military and aerospace technology of all kinds (including, yes, landing on meteorites, traveling to Mars, and returning to the moon), and in information technology. These are the sectors of our global economy that will most drive our futures. And we must lead in everything that determines America's future.

We must be the innovation powerhouse of the twenty-first century to ensure rising standards of living for this generation and those that follow. We must rigorously protect our intellectual property—that produced by the individual inventor as much as that produced by the global powerhouse—and recognize that nations like China are hell-bent on stealing it.

Finally, we must restore American leadership in the

world. We cannot rush to war, but we know that peace and stability in the world require American strength and the power to back it up. We must have indisputable military superiority.

American leadership allows us to control our own destiny. It gives us the ability to influence the rest of the world's direction and agenda. It has costs, of course. It requires a willingness to confront our adversaries and support our allies.

The world needs American leadership—it seems like an obvious statement, but not everyone agrees. The world is a better place when America is leading, and it's a more dangerous place when we fail to lead. Leadership in this context requires a commander in chief who is willing to say, without apology or equivocation, that this is the greatest nation the world has ever known. It's not a question of jingoism but of confidence in ourselves and our principles. We are a force for good in the world because of our principles. Effective American leadership requires moral clarity, clear-eyed realism, the courage to act, and the wisdom to know when it is time for action.

Moral clarity demands that we acknowledge that although some things are gray, some things are black and white. When we are morally ambivalent, we create problems in the world. For example, there is no moral equivalence between Hamas using its citizens as human shields and Israel defending itself. There is no moral equivalence between Ukraine's right to sovereignty and Vladimir Putin's push to restore the Soviet empire. ISIS is evil, and we have to destroy them. Period.

We must be clear-eyed about the nature of the threats we face. We have to acknowledge, for example, that Iran wants a nuclear weapon and will do anything to get it. China is a state sponsor of cyberterrorism, as are Russia and North Korea. It is no coincidence that America suffered a series of cyber-attacks on our banks around the time we were leveling modest sanctions on Russia. We have to be clear-eyed and realistic about what we need to do to protect our interests. Equally important, we have to be clear-eyed and realistic about what we *won't* do. We must have the most prepared, mightiest military in the world to maintain our security. However, we don't need to be in the business of nation building. It was clear-eyed and realistic to go into Afghanistan to destroy safe havens for terrorists. It was not realistic to try to build a central government where none has existed for two thousand years.

The courage to act must be accompanied by the wisdom to know when to act. Put more prosaically, timing is everything. If you want to deter aggression, you have to act in a serious manner when aggression is contemplated, not when it has already occurred. It's not clear that President Obama understands this. The time to level punishing sanctions on Russia, for example, was when it first looked threateningly at Crimea, not after they shot a passenger plane out of the sky. The Obama administration prides itself on being deliberative, and so it should.

Putin's invasion of Crimea, however, was not a surprise. Neither was the rise of ISIS. Leadership requires anticipation and planning for threats. And then, if necessary, action before small threats become big ones.

American leadership also demands that our officials know the difference between the time for talk and the time for action. Our current president confuses the two. He seems to think that if he's talking, he's acting. Talk is only valuable, though, if it signals intent to act. The president seems to think that if he condemns Russia for invading Ukraine or ISIS for beheading James Foley, he has acted. He hasn't. He's just talked.

It is on this point—the difference between talking and acting—that not just President Obama but our politics in general have let the American people down. We live in the era of the professional politician. It used to be that Americans from all walks of life moved in and out of politics. Today, our leaders are for the most part lawyers by training and politicians for life. Many of them are well-intentioned, good people. But their training in the law and experience in government have taught them that talking is acting. Indeed, in the courtroom and in the legislature, speaking and acting can be synonymous.

For those of us from outside government and the legal profession, however, real results are not the product of just words and intentions but of actions and consequences. To get a product to market or launch an innovation requires moving from point A to point B—from the goal to the result. It involves not just acting yourself but motivating others. And crucially, it involves accountability for your actions.

Hillary Clinton confuses talking and acting as well. As secretary of state, Mrs. Clinton reminds us, she flew hundreds of thousands of miles and visited many countries. But what was achieved? Surveying her tenure, she does not list accomplishments, only activities. And when Mrs. Clinton angrily replies, "What difference at this point does it make?" when repeatedly asked about her comments that the Benghazi attacks were prompted by an anti-Muslim video, she reveals how little she understands about restoring American leadership. A deliberate attack by terrorists on our embassy, the deliberate murder of our ambassador and three other Americans—these acts demand a completely different response from America than to brush them off as a spontaneous demonstration gone bad. The fact that America has not responded at all—other than to arrest one perpetrator and bring him to the United States for trial—has emboldened our enemies and disheartened our allies. Our nation's standing in the world is weaker because Secretary Clinton and President Obama missed the moment to lead.

Contrast this with a leader like Ronald Reagan. President Reagan had a vision for ending the Soviet Union as a threat to the United States. He not only communicated this vision, he supported the Strategic Defense Initiative (SDI) in the face of widespread condemnation and ridicule. His action, however, helped produce a result. The Soviet Union couldn't keep up with American military technical prowess and eventually fell.

Finally, leaders know that every problem is also an opportunity. America faces problems with Russia. Therein lies an opportunity to rebuild NATO as well as to reinforce and reestablish European and missile defense systems. The world faces global threats from Iran and ISIS. Nothing is more clarifying than common enemies, and we now have the opportunity to rebuild strained relationships in the Middle East. Jordan, the United Arab Emirates, Qatar, Egypt, Iraq, Saudi Arabia, even Israel—these are all nations with tremendous differences, suspicions, and, in some cases, enmities. Yet when faced with a common threat, these nations have certain shared interests. With American leadership, these shared interests can become common ground.

Our goals, then, are clear: Unlock the potential of every American. Revitalize Main Street and the middle class. Rebuild and retrain America. Reform government. Restore American leadership. The question becomes, how do we organize ourselves to achieve them?

Structures and Processes

Although most Americans will agree on these goals, many perhaps will differ over how to achieve them. This is why an understanding of the double helix of technology and globalization is so important. In truth, only certain things will work these days. Only decentralized decision making will work when centralized bureaucracies inevitably fail. People will, over time, demand more and more choice and more and more control over every aspect of their lives when technology provides them with both of these things every day of their lives. And in an era when the brain power that comes from unlocked human potential is the only reliable tool we have to control our destiny, making government smaller and less powerful so that individuals can become larger and more powerful is the only rational approach.

I became a conservative out of conviction, rather than simply by upbringing, when I realized that conservative solutions work better to solve problems and unlock potential. If the twenty-first century should be the American century, it can only be so if we rediscover the virtues of conservative solutions.

When we consider how we should organize ourselves to achieve our objectives, we inevitably must confront the dissolution or decentralization of many centralized government programs. This is not to suggest that government has no role. Government's rightful role has never been to control others' lives or opportunities. Government's role is to provide the environment in which "life, liberty and the pursuit of happiness" can be best pursued by all Americans. To do so in a DMVP world requires conservative principles.

We must begin a systematic reexamination of every government program and every law and regulation on the books. Today the burden of proof rests on those who want to eliminate a law or a regulation. We should reverse this and require that the burden of proof fall to those who want to keep a program, a law, or a regulation. Argue your case and please present evidence for why it is necessary. The truth is we haven't had a complete inventory of all our programs, laws, and regulations in so long, my guess is we will discover many that have no constituency at all.

We must push as many programs and as much decision making to the states as possible—because the closer decision making is to those most affected by it, the more accountable and effective those decisions will be. Besides, states have to balance their budgets, and this has a sobering effect on those who would argue that every program is indispensable and no dollar can be saved.

Citizens also need to know how their money is being spent. Today, we don't have a clue, and the appropriations process really only examines new programs and questions rates of increase in annual budgets. Anyone who has ever contracted with the federal government knows that every agency routinely spends all of its remaining budget in the last six to eight weeks of the fiscal year—whether they need to or not. This ensures that the only questions asked are about how much more money an agency requests—never what the budget should actually be. There are a lot of ideas about how to change the appropriations process and finally get control of an obviously out-of-control federal budget ($18 trillion in debt and counting). There are merits to all of them. My suggestion would be to engage in true zero-based budgeting every two years; that is, each and every agency must present to Congress where every single dollar is being spent and why. On the table for discussion: every program and every dollar, rather than just the rate of increase over the previous year. And in the DMVP age, every agency owes to the public an annual report that details every program and every taxpayer dollar spent.

Metrics and Rewards

Next is the issue of how we will measure our progress. In particular, how do we define and reward success?

The answer is to rebuild government bureaucracies into meritocracies. There are many highly intelligent, well-intended people in government. But when there is no reward for standout performance and no penalty for nonperformance, these hardworking civil servants cannot be recognized or their talents leveraged. The civil service needs to become a pay-for-performance environment.

Today we celebrate the passage of laws and we comment on the writing of regulations. We need to begin rewarding repeals and eliminations. Let's reward the consolidation of programs. Let's celebrate collaboration across bureaucracies rather than reward those who jealously guard their turf. Let's measure how many new businesses are created every day. Let's publicize patent production across our country. In other words, measuring and rewarding things tends to create more of that thing. Bill Hewlett used to say: "What gets measured is what gets done." It is true. People assume you are measuring something because it is valued. So let's measure and reward and recognize the things we value: consolidation, elimination, savings. Senator Tom Coburn should be lauded as a hero and thanked by every American for his unflagging exposure of waste, fraud, and corruption in the federal government.

Every government program should be reimagined in a DMVP age. The questions we should always ask are: If we were starting over, and had nothing in place, how would we deliver this benefit to these citizens in the most efficient and effective way possible? What information would we ask citizens to provide from their cell phones? How would we authenticate their identity? How could we deliver benefits to them through technology? When you consider that at Opportunity International we can deliver a loan to a woman living in destitute circumstances through mobile banking on a cell phone, it is beyond absurd that here, in the richest nation on earth, our veterans must fill out reams of paperwork and wait for months as their paperwork is reviewed just to receive benefits they have already earned in service to our country. The truth about technology systems is this: it is always easier, cheaper, and faster to start over than to try to fix what has been in place for decades. We need to "greenfield" our government's technology rather than spending decades trying to fix what can never be adequately repaired.

In the DMVP age, technology can be our friend in many ways. It can smash hierarchies by ensuring that every citizen has access to as much information as possible about what is actually going on in government. From such transparency comes accountability. When people know what is happening, they tend to look for who is responsible. A focus on accountability can accelerate an emphasis on performance and results.

People want choices and control in their lives. Competition and free markets—not crony capitalism—can provide both. I come from the technology industry. It is arguably the most hypercompetitive and least-regulated industry in the world. It is also the one area in the global economy where every year, year after year, customers see real innovation, real new value, better quality, and lower prices. This is not a coincidental relationship. It is cause and effect. We should use these same principles to truly reform health care and education. Government bureaucracies cannot improve either—they will only create more problems for more people.

As we undertake the difficult but necessary and overdue work of reforming and reducing the federal government, we should remember that this will take much time and strong leadership. The inevitable resistance to this great challenge and the mind-numbing complexity of the task will dishearten and discourage even the strongest at times. When people begin to question—as they invariably do when the going gets tough—whether this is all really necessary or even doable, it's important to remember the basics: centralized bureaucracies will always fail in a DMVP era. Human potential is a limitless resource that must be unlocked, focused, and leveraged to solve our problems and tap into our opportunities.

Culture and Behavior

The last parameter of systemic change is around culture and behavior. What do we value? How do we behave? Changing culture truly requires a long-term effort and cannot be driven from the top down but rather must be supported from the bottom up. Yet here, too, I believe most Americans agree on the basics.

Americans of all ages and ethnicities realize that we cannot focus solely on short-term satisfaction; we must have longer-term goals and vision. Americans are tired of being used in a political game. They are tired of the ad wars, the vitriol, and the sound bites. They want reasoned, respectful conversations about the issues that confront us all. Although the perpetual campaign may serve politics, it no longer serves the people. At some point, people know the campaigning needs to stop and the real work needs to begin.

Most Americans know that self-indulgence is both overrated and overcelebrated. We celebrate the brash and the outrageous. And yet people instinctively are touched and respond to the humility and self-restraint exemplified by Pope Francis. We have too many with the ambition to succeed in politics, and too few with the desire to serve. We honor our nation's veterans because we know valor, service, and sacrifice when we see them, and we deeply appreciate these qualities. We can encourage and reward people all over America for engaging in service of many kinds in their communities. For example, rather than dismiss the work of millions of women who volunteer in local charities every day, we should hold them up as heroes in our nation.

While we have become politically correct to a fault, too many of our political leaders don't really reward or encourage true respect for others. I can remember a donor to my Senate campaign telling me, "You can't really be pro-life. You're a Stanford and MIT graduate!" Translation: you must be stupid to be pro-life. When the debate over "marriage equality" comes up, someone inevitably remarks that those who don't support gay marriage lack compassion. Tea Partiers are called racist. Nancy Pelosi castigates the GOP as "the party of Ray Rice." President Obama routinely describes those who disagree with him as venal, self-serving, lacking in intelligence, or all of the above. And on the conservative side, our tone and language matter just as much. Whatever we suppose the solutions are to the immigration crisis, calling people "aliens" is disrespectful. Dismissing 47 percent of Americans as takers whom we should write off in our political efforts is disrespectful. An unwillingness to engage with people simply because they have not supported our candidates in the past is self-defeating as well as disrespectful.

Of course, most of the media encourage the discord and the potshots. Conflict is news, and nasty conflict is big news. All of this not only cheapens our political discourse, it discourages mutual respect and civility. Leaders set a tone for culture.

Our culture is damaged most when faith is driven from the public square and discouraged in public discourse. I am a Christian, but I respect sincere people of every faith. We should celebrate true faith of all kinds—as distinguished from the perversion of faith into political doctrine or militant ideology—as a virtue. Rather than discouraging a reliance on God for wisdom and guidance, we should acknowledge that people of faith make better leaders. Faith gives us humility. We know that we are all equal in the eyes of God and that He alone is great. Faith gives us empathy. We know that any one of us can fall and that each of us can be redeemed. Faith gives us optimism. We know that people can lift others up and be lifted up themselves. We know there is a better place. We know there is a plan—even if we cannot see or understand it. We know there is hope.

The highest calling of leadership is to unlock potential in others. Leaders who undertake to change the order of things pray often. We pray for forgiveness and grace. We pray for guidance and wisdom. We pray for endurance and strength. We need more prayer in American life, not less.

■ ■ ■

In the twenty-first century, this new age of technology and globalization, of danger and possibility, of opportunity and challenge, we must remember who we are. When fundamental reform and systemic change is required—and it is most definitely required in Washington, D.C.—it is vital to also reinforce what still remains true and what is core to our national character. We are a resilient nation and a generous people. We are adaptable, determined, persistent, and capable. We celebrate the individual, rather than the collective, and we celebrate when individuals join together in effective teams. We are risk takers. We are builders. We are brave and we are honorable. We pursue lives of dignity, purpose, and meaning for ourselves and our families. We appreciate self-reliance, and we appreciate the impact and import of charity as well. All these qualities are at the heart of who we are.

And so I return to the hollow-eyed men in the town of Mendota, California. With their potential crushed as their livelihoods were destroyed, with their hopes dashed by nameless, faceless bureaucrats thousands of miles away, they lost the essence of who they are as Americans. They were no longer self-reliant risk takers building a future for their families. They no longer felt brave in the face of a crushing force they could not understand. They did not know how to adapt when they saw water running through their communities—water that could save their orchards, their jobs, and their lives—but water they could not use. Of all the things I resent most about out-of-control government and the politicians who support it, grow it, or simply fail to deal with it, what angers me above all else is the knowledge that all of this waste and ruin is entirely preventable.

Americans know we are losing something. We are losing a sense of limitless possibility. This, too, is the essence of who we are. We have always been a nation that believed everything is possible and that we could, and would, do it all.

Americans know we are missing something. What we are missing is leadership, the kind of leadership that knows its highest calling is to unlock the potential of every American and restore the possibilities for this great nation. Here everyone deserves a chance, and anyone can achieve their aspirations.

It is time. It is time to end the era of big government

once and for all. It is time to return to citizen government and reasoned debate. It is time to declare the end of class warfare, the end of identity politics, the end of lowered expectations.

This is the greatest nation the world has ever known. And so we must, together, undertake the difficult but necessary work to restore our nation's promise. Together we must lead our nation to fulfill our potential. Let us rise to meet our destiny and be the nation we must be.

With God's continued blessings and the unbroken spirit of the American people, we will.

Epilogue

MY FIRST BOOK, *TOUGH CHOICES*, BEGAN with my mother and father. This book will end with them.

Perhaps this is because as we grow older and, hopefully, wiser, we appreciate even more keenly the power and exceptional nature of timeless values. From my mother I learned that we are all uniquely gifted by God and that our life's journey is about discovering and using these gifts to their fullest. From my father I learned that character is the core of who we are and the foundation of what we can become. Integrity is defined by what we do, how we act, what we choose, how we decide—especially when no one is looking or when we have the power to do whatever we like. Both my parents believed that no one of us is better than any other; so although self-respect and self-confidence are important, humility and respect for others are required in equal measure.

Over the course of my life I have learned three more profound lessons. First, the highest calling of leadership is to unlock potential in others, and everyone is capable of such leadership. Second, from my battle with cancer, I have come to know that life is not measured in time. It is measured instead in love, positive contribution, and moments of grace. And with the death of our beloved Lori, I came to know that we control nothing but our own choices. Our lives come down to how we choose to use our gifts and our character.

I know that my story and my life are only possible in the United States of America. It is only here that a young woman, a law school dropout and a secretary, can go on to become the chief executive of the largest technology company in the world and have the opportunities and the privileges that I have experienced. And that is because the Founders knew what my mother taught me: everyone has God-given gifts, and everyone should have the chance to use them.

Our Founders knew that every life has potential—to invent, to create, to make the world better, to live a life of dignity and purpose and meaning. This is what they meant when they wrote "life, liberty and the pursuit of happiness." Our Founders also knew that for human potential to be fulfilled, the use of power must be re-strained lest it be abused.

As I have lived and worked, I have seen over and over that human potential is the only limitless resource we have. When it is unlocked, focused on worthy goals and common purpose, then truly everything is possible. Yet it is also true that potential cannot be fulfilled unless the rule of law prevails; the rule of law holds accountable the most powerful among us and protects even those who are powerless.

Our Founders intended that laws should be relatively difficult to enact, requiring careful deliberation and some degree of consensus achieved among representatives of the people. They knew, as I have come to know over a lifetime of experience, that it is a fine line between the rule of law that enables, empowers, and unleashes human potential, and a heavy-handed crushing of the entrepreneurial and innovative spirit. Human potential is crushed when some—who think they know better than others—decide that their job is to direct the activities of others, redirect the decisions of others, or to take matters into their own hands that rightly belong to others.

We celebrate our Founding Fathers, wise men all, who wrote the Constitution to prevent the crushing of the human spirit through the abuse of power. Still, among the most powerful symbols of our nation are two women: Lady Liberty and Lady Justice. Lady Liberty stands clear-eyed and resolute, her torch held high, a beacon of hope in a weary world. She faces outward into that world, as America always must, because the world needs our leadership and is a sadder and more dangerous place when we turn away. We see that she is strong and brave and leads the way.

And then there is Lady Justice, with her blindfold and her sword. Do you imagine someone put the blindfold on her? Unlikely—she, after all, is the one with the sword. If she wears a blindfold, it is because she put it on herself. She was not born blind, any more than she was born armed. However, in order to ignore what cannot matter to the law, she takes up that limitation when she takes up the sword to restrict the power of the state within clear bounds. We take Lady Justice now as the symbol of impartiality. Properly understood, however, she is more. She represents limited government, limited by her own restraint.

James Madison wrote in *Federalist No. 55* that whatever prudent safeguards we might devise, government in our republic would still make great demands on the integrity and devotion to duty of officeholders, the personal virtues and character appropriate to self-government that require, first of all, the capacity to govern oneself. This sort of restraint does not come from a grudging sacrifice or asceticism, although tough choices are inevitable. Constitutional fidelity is a positive virtue, not a negative one, and it is rooted in love for the law and for this country that overcomes any temptation to depart from it. Constitutional fidelity comes from humility. It comes as well from a profound appreciation that human potential is a powerful force for progress—if it is guided by the wisdom and experience of the many, not directed by the decisions of the few. In other words, real freedom—the kind of freedom that unlocks potential for progress, for daring, for doing, for dreaming—requires real restraint and real humility.

I got involved in politics when I realized that the policies politicians choose affect our lives in profound ways. Politics is also something within our power to change. To do so, we must make the case for humility and restraint in a way that transcends our national division between right and left. We have to break free of the persistent narrative that reduces constitutional principles to just the usual battles between Republicans and Democrats. What we know, but some liberal ideologues do not (or worse, know but refuse to acknowledge), is that the fundamental contest of ideas in which we are engaged is far more profound and fundamental than partisan politics.

Our nation was founded on the visionary idea that everyone has potential and that everyone should have the right to fulfill that potential. To preserve these possibilities for future generations, to unleash the potential of every American and of our great nation in the twenty-first century, a love for the Constitution and the free society it envisions must become the bedrock commitment for more of our legal community, our legislators, and our presidents. It must be spread widely among all our citizens as part of the very meaning of citizenship.

My life's experiences as a leader and a problem solver, the wisdom of my mother and father, my battle with cancer, and the too-soon death of our daughter Lori have taught me that our freedom to make choices is both precious and powerful. Let us continue together to talk to all Americans with the daring and inspirational message of the founding generation. Let us together pledge ourselves to the renewal of our nation and to the preservation for our own children and grandchildren of the greatest privilege a people has ever been granted: the opportunity to rule ourselves.

Acknowledgments

READERS OF *TOUGH CHOICES* WILL REMEMBER that I was hesitant to write that first book. And so it was with this, my second. My husband, Frank, has never wavered in his conviction that *Rising to the Challenge* should be written. Nevertheless, this is a story about him and Lori as well as me and it is deeply personal. His unwavering love and faith in me have been the touchstone of my life. His willingness to allow me to share our story is an act of generosity for which I am forever grateful.

Adrian Zackheim believed in the first book and believed in this one. His enthusiastic support has made all the difference.

Jessica Gavora was a true partner, helping me think through the structure and the content of *Rising to the Challenge*. I enjoyed our collaboration tremendously.

Finally, while writing this book, I would think of all the people I have met and heard from in the last decade. I have always drawn my energy from people—their stories, their struggles, their aspirations. I draw inspiration from them as well and am blessed to have encountered so many who have lifted me up.

Index

abortion, 136–37
accountability, 13, 66–67, 94, 150,
    185
ACU Foundation, 141
Advani, Ranjana, 68–69, 71–72
Advisory Committee for
    Transformational Diplo-
    macy, 43, 44–45
Affordable Care Act
    (Obamacare), 165
Afghanistan, invasion of, 168
African Leadership Academy,
    149
American Conservative Union
    (ACU), 141–42
American Dream, 10–12, 51, 87,
    122, 132

American economy:
    decline of, 160–61
    free market capitalism, 15, 176
    national debt, 112, 160
    stimulus bill, 67, 98, 110–11,
        164
    unemployment, 109, 110, 112
    wages, 42
Astorino, Rob, 135–36

Bayer, Michael, 43
Bhutto, Benazir, 148
Biden, Jill, 116
Biden, Joe, 53, 116
bitcoin, 155
Blackburn, Marsha, 49

Bowker, Deborah, 58, 61–62, 68,
        70, 78, 79, 91, 115, 116
Boxer, Barbara, 139
    and California drought, 104–6
    and Senate campaign, 54–56,
        63, 64, 76, 77, 79–80, 88, 91,
        94–95, 97–100, 101–2,
        107–14, 116, 117, 118
Brem, Rachel, 75
Brown, Jerry, 81, 112, 128
Brown, Scott, 93
Brownback, Sam, 139
Buchanan, Brooke, 47
bureaucracies:
    centralized, 172
    change as difficult in, 45–46
    in education, 160
    failures of, 165–66, 172
    government-related, 43–45,
        111, 126, 128–29
    hierarchies in, 165
    human potential crushed by,
        16–17, 20, 132, 146, 181
    measurement of, 174–77
    Pentagon, 45
    rules and regulations of, 127
    self-preservation of, 19–20, 126,
        161
    seniority system in, 145
Bush, George W., 25, 27, 28

California:
    budget deficit of, 64
    cautionary tale of, 120–27, 132
    education in, 125–26, 129
    entrepreneurship in, 67–68

    exodus from, 122–26
    jobs in, 109, 111
    leadership in, 88, 132
    middle class driven from,
        64–65, 122–26, 128
    misery in, 129–30, 132
    parable of, 157–58
    reform in, 128–29
    Republican Convention, 58, 63,
        64, 66–68, 99
    taxes in, 124–26, 127
    technology companies in,
        120–21
    water in, 102–7
    wealth gap in, 127–28
Campbell, Tom, 91–96, 99–101
cancer, 57–76, 77, 81–82, 87–88,
        96–97, 115–16, 184
capitalism:
    crony, 20, 52, 99, 176
    free market, 15, 176
Carlson, Norm, 22
Carlson, Robert, 72
Carly Fiorina Enterprises, 61
Central Intelligence Agency
        (CIA), 43, 44
Central Valley, California, 102–7,
        121–22
challenge, systemic approaches
        to, 161
Chambliss, Saxby, 113
Chicago Teachers Union, 131
children:
    care of, 131–32
    of poverty, 131
China:
    cyberterrorism in, 168

education of, 159–60
technological theft in, 166
Climate Resilience Fund, 107
Clinton, Hillary, 14, 49, 170
Common Core, 159
Conservative Political Action
     Conference (CPAC), 142
conservative solutions, 172–73
Constitutional fidelity, 186–87
Cornyn, John, 113
crony capitalism, 20, 52, 99, 176
Cuomo, Andrew, 135, 137

Davis, Fred, 79, 95, 99
de Blasio, Bill, 131
Defense Business Board, 43, 45
Defense Department, U.S., 43, 45
delta smelt, 102–3
DeMint, Jim, 105
"demon sheep" video, 95–96
Department of National Intelli-
     gence, 44
Devore, Chuck, 91–93, 95, 111
Dirbas, Fred, 72
Disaster Recovery360, 18
DMVP (Digital, Mobile, Virtual,
     Personal), 154–56, 165, 172,
     174, 175, 176
Dodd-Frank Act (2010), 51
dot-com bubble, collapse of, 26

Earth Friendly Products, 87
Ebola crisis, 17–18
education, 13, 15, 42–43, 109, 131,
     157, 158–60, 164

Edusave, 150
Edwards, Elizabeth, 75
Einstein, Albert, 86
El-Bayoumi, Gigi, 74
Emanuel, Rahm, 13
empowerment, 21–22
Endangered Species Act, 103, 105
Engler, John, 43
entrepreneurship, 15–16, 22,
     67–68, 98, 150, 158, 185
Escarra, Vicki, 150

faith, 4–5, 84–86, 179–80
Federal Emergency Management
     Agency (FEMA), 19
Federalist Papers, 186–87
Feinstein, Dianne, 92, 105
feminist movement, 38
financial crisis (2007–2008),
     50–53
Fiorina, Carly:
   cancer battle of, 6–7, 57–76, 77,
     81–82, 87–88, 96–97, 115–16,
     184
   and her parents, 86, 183–84,
     188
   and HP, *see* Hewlett-Packard
   as public speaker, 9–12, 31–34,
     35, 40–41, 66–68, 153–54
   Senate candidacy of, 54–56, 65,
     70, 76, 77–82, 87, 88, 91–118
   Tough Choices, 32, 34–38, 39, 40,
     42, 66, 162, 183
Fiorina, Frank, 27, 34, 36
   and author's campaigns, 87,
     116, 117–18

Fiorina, Frank (*cont.*)
  and author's cancer, 62–63, 68,
    69, 71, 115
  birthday celebration of, 89–90
  and Lori's death, 1–2, 5, 84, 86
Fiorina, Kara and Morgan
  (granddaughters), 34, 119
Fiorina, Lori, 1–7, 23, 34, 82–86,
  90, 184, 188
Fiorina, Tracy, 34, 84, 90, 119
Foley, James, 169
Founding Fathers, 130, 184–85
Francis, Pope, 178
Frank, Barney, 125
freedom, 16

Gaba, Nancy, 75
Gates, Robert M., 43, 45
General Motors, 52
Giuliani, Rudy, 132
globalization, 42, 153, 155–57,
  166, 172, 180
Good360, 17–19
government:
  bureaucracy of, 43–45, 111, 126,
    128–29
  and business, 66, 88, 110
  complete inventory of, 173–74
  dissatisfaction with, 93, 99, 125,
    158
  and education, 160
  national debt, 112, 160
  reelection as goal in, 137
  reform needed in, 164–65
  roles of, 14, 98, 172
  self-government, 186–87, 188

stimulus bill, 67, 98, 110–11, 164
  and water, 103–7
government bailouts, 50–51, 52
Graham, Lindsey, 113
Greenberg, Lauren, 72, 115
Gruber, Jonathan, 129–30, 131

Halberlin, Cindy, 19
Hayden, Michael, 43, 44
Hewlett, Bill, 41, 120, 175
Hewlett-Packard (HP):
  author as CEO of, 30, 42, 43, 79,
    108, 113, 114
  author's departure from,
    25–27, 29, 30, 31, 32, 33,
    36–37, 75–76
  board of directors, 28–29, 31,
    38–40
  bureaucracy of, 42, 114
  "HP way" in, 41–42
  innovation in, 41
  Leadership Framework in,
    162–63
  start-up of, 120
  and taxes, 66
Hilton, Paris, 79
hopelessness, 5–6, 7, 12–13, 23,
  104, 181
human potential:
  and American Dream, 10–12,
    87, 132
  bureaucratic limits on, 16–17,
    20, 132, 146, 181
  and entrepreneurship, 15–16
  Founders' recognition of, 130,
    184–85

and free markets, 15
as limitless resource, 185
most precious asset of, 157,
    160
power of, 13–14, 46, 187
unlocking, 14–16, 20–22, 68,
    153–56, 164, 184, 187–88
humility, 187
Hunt, Gary, 78
Hutchison, Kay Bailey, 78
Hybels, Bill, 85

"I'm Free" (anon.), 83–84
immigration law, 130, 138, 164,
    179
innovation, 166
Internet:
    advertising on, 95–96
    taxation of, 66
iPhone, 155
Iran, threats from, 171
ISIS, rise of, 169, 171

jobs, 109–12
    competition for, 156–57
    creation of, 95, 98, 110, 111,
        114
    destruction of, 104, 109
    dignity in work, 16
    and education, 109, 157
    moved overseas, 42, 127
    qualified applicants lacking
        for, 164
    and stimulus bill, 110–11
Jobs, Steve, 27, 30

Kennedy, Ted, 93
Keystone XL pipeline, 110
Khachigian, Ken, 101
Kissinger, Henry A., 49
Kotkin, Joel, 124, 129

Lady Justice, 185–86
Lady Liberty, 185–86
leadership:
    anticipation needed in, 169
    essence of, 41, 42–43
    in global economy, 166
    highest calling of, 184
    lack of, 122, 132, 181
    potential unlocked via, 20–22,
        68, 184
    and prosperity, 114
    requirements of, 167
    restoration of, 166–67
    teaching, 149
Leadership Framework, 161–63
    culture and behavior, 177–80
    goals and strategy, 163–71
    metrics and rewards, 174–77
    questions asked in, 162–63
    structure and process, 171–74
liberal ideology, 129–31, 132,
    137

MadgeTech, 22
Madison, James, 186
McCain, John, 46–50, 52–53, 81,
    113, 137
McConnell, Mitch, 113
measurement, 174–77

media, discord promoted by, 179

Mendota, California, hopeless-ness in, 5–6, 12, 23, 102, 103–4, 106, 181

midterm elections (2014), 142

Mody, Arjun, 79

moral clarity, 167–68

Most Powerful Women Summit, San Diego, 74–75

music industry, 154

national debt, 112, 160

National Intelligence Estimate on Iran, 44

National Republican Senatorial Committee (NRSC), 113

National Right to Life Commit-tee, 100

NATO, 171

New Hampshire Rotary Club, author's speech to, 9–12

Nixon, Richard M., 101

North Carolina A&T, author's speech to, 31–34, 35

North Korea, 168

Nunes, Devin, 121

Obama, Barack, 14, 49, 53, 65, 79, 93, 106–7, 116, 130, 168, 169–70, 178

Obama, Michelle, 116

Obama administration, 97–98, 110, 168

Obamacare, 69–70, 130, 146, 165

One Woman Initiative, 148–49

opportunity, 15, 21–22, 66, 67–68

Opportunity International (OI), 149–52, 175

Packard, Dave, 41, 120

Palin, Sarah, 48–50, 52–53, 100, 113

Paulson, Henry, 50

Poizner, Steve, 92

politics:
    effect on our lives, 46, 187
    grassroots, 141–43
    paucity of results in, 140
    professionals in, 169
    sound bites of, 161
    vitriol in, 140

pretexting, 39

Putin, Vladimir, 167–68, 169

Reagan, Ronald, 54, 101, 116, 121, 142, 170–71

Remy and Amina, story of, 151–52

Rice, Condoleezza, 43, 44, 148

Roosevelt, Theodore, 120

Rose, Charlie, 49

rule of law, 185

Rumsfeld, Donald, 43

Russia, 168, 171

Schwarzenegger, Arnold, 79

September 11 attacks, 26

Serenity Prayer, 83

sexism, 26–27, 37–38, 49

small business, 20, 66, 111, 122, 158, 164
Soderland, Julie, 79, 116
Spears, Britney, 79
Spencer, Barb, 116
Spencer, Karen, 116
Spencer, Stu, 116–17
Steel, Shawn, 53–54
Strategic Defense Initiative, 170
Sundheim, Duf, 54
Susan B. Anthony List, 100
Swift, Jane, 49

Teal, Christine, 75
Tea Party, 91, 93
technology, 153–57, 172, 180
  change impelled by, 156–57
  DMVP, 154–56, 176
  economic effects of, 42
Thatcher, Margaret, 21
Thune, John, 113
Todd, Chuck, 138
tooth-to-tail ratio, 45
Tough Choices (Fiorina), 32, 34–38, 39, 40, 42, 66, 162, 183
Troubled Assets Relief Program (TARP), 51

Unlocking Potential Project (UP), 144–48

Veterans Administration, 165
Virginia, Fiorinas' move to, 119–20

Vlahakis, Van, 87
Voegeli, William, 125
volunteerism, 139–40, 147

Walsh, Michael, 80
Warren, Elizabeth, 127–28
water, 102–7, 181
Watson, Sarah, 58–61, 63
wealth gap, 127–28
Whitman, Meg, 80–81, 92, 108, 112
Wilson, Marty, 79, 95, 116
Winfrey, Oprah, 27, 37
women, 135–52
  and abortion, 136–37
  apathy of, 140
  and children, 131–32
  community captains, 147
  disengagement of, 140
  equal pay for, 144–45
  and feminist movement, 38
  financial hardships of, 37–38
  at grassroots, 141, 143
  issues that matter to, 144–45, 147
  labor force participation of, 145
  marginalization of, 37–38, 148
  myths about, 144
  phony war on, 142–45, 147–48
  and politics, 135, 136, 142–44, 147–48
  potential of, 140–41, 147
  and poverty, 131, 145, 151
  and seniority system, 145

women (*cont.*)
    as single parents, 146
    social media used by, 147
    suffering of, 139, 147
    volunteers, 139–40, 145, 147
Women's Equality Act, 135–37,
    144–45

work:
    dignity in, 16
    unemployment, 109, 110, 112
    see also jobs

Zackheim, Adrian, 34, 35–36